Religion in
Composition C

Religion in the Composition Classroom

A Pragmatic Approach

Joe Wagner

McFarland & Company, Inc., Publishers
Jefferson, North Carolina

LIBRARY OF CONGRESS CATALOGUING-IN-PUBLICATION DATA

Wagner, Joe, 1968–
    Religion in the composition classroom : a pragmatic approach /
Joe Wagner.
        p.   cm.
    Includes bibliographical references and index.

    ISBN 978-0-7864-7835-4 (softcover : acid free paper) ∞
    ISBN 978-1-4766-2055-8 (ebook)

    1. Religious literature—Authorship.   2. English language—
Rhetoric—Study and teaching.   I. Title.

BL41.W34 2015
200.71'1—dc23   2015017397

BRITISH LIBRARY CATALOGUING DATA ARE AVAILABLE

Front cover image © Wavebreak Media/Thinkstock

Printed in the United States of America

McFarland & Company, Inc., Publishers
  Box 611, Jefferson, North Carolina 28640
    www.mcfarlandpub.com

For Sonia and Isabel

Acknowledgments

This book would not have been possible without the help of so many people. I am indebted to Sherrie Gradin, my professor at Ohio University, who introduced me to the field of composition and rhetoric and encouraged my initial interest in this topic. Hepsie Roskelly then helped me to further refine my thinking in Greensboro, where I also received invaluable advice from Nancy Myers and Ali Schultheis. I want to thank the editors at *Writing on the Edge* for giving me permission to use parts of my article "God in the Comp Class: A Pragmatic Approach" (20:1 2009). I am grateful, as well, for the detailed advice I received from my anonymous peer reviewers. I want to thank, especially, the ten students who were kind enough to let me use their work in this project. And finally, without the constant help and support of my family—my mom and dad, my brother and sister, my wife Sonia, and our three-year-old daughter Isabel (who offered some late-night advice)—this book would not exist.

Table of Contents

Preface

The aim of this book is to help us work with religion as a subject of inquiry in the first-year composition course. It draws on central ideas from American pragmatists like Charles Peirce, William James and John Dewey to frame an approach that combines real-world experience, active reflection, possibility, usefulness, and mediation (as opposed to compromise). As James wrote, religious belief is exactly the kind of thing that pragmatism was designed for: "the pragmatic method is primarily a method of settling metaphysical disputes that otherwise might be interminable" (*Pragmatism* 23). The book also draws on more than a decade of my experience teaching composition in both Chile and the United States, and incorporates real-world events such as Chile's own September 11 in 1973, the recent resignation of Pope Benedict XVI, and daily negotiations of religious belief between family members. It includes, as well, a number of literary references both to help demonstrate the pragmatic method I describe and to serve as material writing teachers might actually use in the classroom when working with religion.

The book offers a number of reading and writing assignments for the composition course, and discusses in some detail ten student essays that take up religious belief. Overall, it moves us to focus on what religious belief does in the world—that is, the tangible consequences of believing or not believing—and steers us away from questions concerning God's existence or benevolence. It invokes both Chilean and American culture, and it highlights connections between the process of writing and how we can work together when it comes to religion. My hope is that the book is useful for anyone teaching composition, but also for anyone outside academia who is interested in a discussion about religion as a social and political force that affects human interaction.

Before we get much further, though, a definition is in order. When

I use the word "religion" and the phrase "religious belief," I am referring to the major monotheistic traditions. I rely mostly upon Roman Catholic and Protestant worldviews as examples for the following reasons: In my experience (both in the U.S. and in Chile), these have been the views I have come across the most in the secular composition course. Also, with respect to religion as a social and political force in the United States, I believe these serve as good illustrations. I take them as examples only, examples of how we can work with any religious belief system in which the supernatural is invoked.

In the introduction, I outline why religious belief should be considered at all in a first-year writing course and how, in this particular context, religion might be different from other topics like race, class, and gender. Then in chapter 1, I introduce the central argument of the book: we can work effectively with religious belief by asking first what it does in the world instead of starting with and wrangling over what we already believe it to be. The chapter suggests how to begin framing that question and it lays the groundwork for why the pragmatists are perfectly suited to help us here. It also explores how private and public worlds interact with one another—a theme developed throughout the book with respect to the writing class. This chapter draws on a number of prominent writers like Susanne Langer, Ralph Waldo Emerson, Marcel Proust, Henry Ward Beecher and James Agee; it draws, too, on my father-in-law's experience after Pinochet's coup in Chile and on the way in which a Chilean married couple negotiates differing views of religious belief.

Chapter 2 describes how three central figures of American Pragmatism understood religion. I focus on Charles Sanders Peirce, the founder of American Pragmatism, William James, the pioneering psychologist who made a special application of Peirce's pragmatism to religious belief, and John Dewey who, rooted in the pragmatism of Peirce and James, helped to transform the country's thinking about education. Taken together, what these three pragmatists have to say about religion can help us work with this intimidating topic in the writing course. In chapter 3, I try to show *how* they can help us by offering some practical guidelines and boundaries. I discuss essays by John Updike and Rachel Carson, offer a number of possible places for us to look when writing about religion, and grapple with issues like habit and authority. I talk, as well, about avoiding the trap of ontological claims.

2

Preface

Chapter 4 is concerned with reading and writing assignments and how we might respond to them in light of our parameters. I discuss a story by Anton Chekhov and several pieces from *The Seagull Reader: Essays*; I look as well to Flannery O'Connor, Katherine Anne Porter, Tony Kushner, movies like *A Time to Kill*, and how we might write about art when it comes to religious belief. The chapter ends by turning to student essays on religion that I have received in my composition courses over the last few years. These essays come from three different assignments often found in the first-year writing course. I explore and include them to provide concrete examples of how the pragmatic approach I describe can aid instructors when students write about religion in various contexts (example essays in their entirety may be found in the Appendix). Finally, in the Conclusion, I return to the notion that religion belongs in the composition course and I emphasize how the approach described in this book can help everyone in the course to work with this complicated subject.

Introduction

The first composition text I used as a new teaching assistant in graduate school has an essay in it by John Updike, an author I felt relatively comfortable with. The essay, though, titled "On Being a Self Forever," revolves around religion. As much as I wanted to include it, opening the door to religious belief seemed more than I was prepared to do. So I left it off the syllabus.

That was about fifteen years ago, and since then a lot has been written about addressing religion in the first-year writing course. Building upon work by composition scholars like Lizabeth Rand, Judson B. Curry, Chris Anderson, and Amy Goodburn who pointed to religion as a valuable topic and resource came, for instance, *The Academy and the Possibility of Belief: Essays on Intellectual and Spiritual Life* by Mary Louise Buly-Meissner, Mary McCaslin Thompson, and Elizabeth Bachrach Tan. Published in 2000, this collection provided a forum for greater "debate and discussion about the best way to educate students concerning religion and spirituality," a debate and discussion that Robert N. Sollod said was "long overdue" (16). In 2005, Elizabeth Vander Lei and bonnie lenore kyburz extended that forum with *Negotiating Religious Faith in the Writing Classroom,* and the subject continues to draw steady attention.

In 2014, though, Thomas Deans suggests that nearly all of this research has focused primarily on "considerations of student texts and their contexts" or taken the form of "case studies, analyses, and reflections published in academic journals and books" (409). While this work has been groundbreaking and is still necessary—I hope to add to it from the lens I propose in this book—Deans would like us to think more about primary texts that, as James Slevin puts it, "'work to construct the subjectivity of writers, readers, [and] educators' or that 'respond thematically or consciously ... to a difficulty of writing'" (409). Deans argues

5

specifically for adding primary sacred texts to the composition canon and offers the biblical story of the woman accused of adultery (John 7.53–8.11) as a compelling example. While I don't offer any primary sacred texts in and of themselves, I try to provide throughout this book a variety of texts that "work to construct the subjectivity" of readers, writers, and educators or that "respond thematically or consciously" to a "difficulty of writing" when it comes to religion. These texts range from popular movies and essays or stories by famous writers to newspaper advertisements, student essays, and Supreme Court decisions.

I step back here a bit to provide a few other points of reference for how I came to think about addressing religious belief in the writing course. In 2008, Stanley Fish published a book entitled *Save the World on Your Own Time*. While Fish has come under attack of late for being out of touch with the first-year composition course (see, for instance, "What Should Colleges Teach" parts 1 through 3), his, I believe, is a valuable voice. In *Save the World*, he makes the argument that far too often we are "giving the writing course over to discussions of various forms of discrimination" and that teachers end up becoming "political agents engaged in political advocacy" rather than teaching the subject for which they were hired (17, 20). In some ways, Fish's book reminded me of an essay written by Maxine Hairston in 1992 titled "Diversity, Ideology, and Teaching Writing." Here, Hairston argues that it's irresponsible to focus on social and political issues like race and gender in the composition class. She warns that we must avoid politicizing this course, refrain from forcing our personal views on our students, and strive to provide a low-risk environment in which they can improve their writing (669, 670). She specifically cautions us against delving into topics that we are not particularly trained for: "We have no business getting into areas where we may have passion and conviction but no scholarly base from which to operate," she argues. "When classes focus on complex issues such as racial discrimination, economic injustices, and inequities of class and gender, they should be taught by qualified faculty who have the depth of information and historical competence that such critical social issues warrant" (667).

Both Fish and Hairston raise valid concerns, as it's not hard to lose sight of the main purpose of this course when the subjects of inquiry can so easily lead us astray. The obvious shouldn't be forgotten: the focus of study in a composition course should be writing, and anything we explore should be used as a means for improving our students' writing. With that in mind, sensitive topics have long found a place near the heart of most composition courses. The market for our textbooks reflects this direction, a direction captured by Keith Gilyard's suggestion in 1996 that "writing is not an activity that features social responsibility as an option. Writing *is* social responsibility. When you write, you are being responsible to some social entity even if that entity is yourself" (21). Underlying this assertion is an ocean of work by John Dewey and many others who have argued that education is necessarily a social entity and should not be seen as something separate from the real world in which we live.

The problem, of course, is *how* subjects of study are addressed in the composition course. Going back to Stanley Fish, in *Save the World*, he asks, "[Do I] mean that questions of value and discussions of current events must be banished from the classroom? Not at all. No question, issue, or topic is off limits to classroom discussion so long as it is the object of academic rather than political or ideological attention" (15). As noted above, religion has increasingly become the subject of academic attention in the field of composition and rhetoric, but in some ways approaching religious belief still prompts a few of those concerns that Hairston raised in the early '90s—as writing teachers we shouldn't be going where we don't belong and where we're not qualified. And in other ways, religious belief presents a peculiar set of problems such as what to do with proselytizing or the various ways our own beliefs/disbeliefs might enter the mix.

Together with these concerns is the fact that religion is not something most writing teachers would be happy to eradicate like racism or sexism. There is a basic understanding (or so we hope) that these "isms" continue to do us no good and that we'd be better off without them. Not all in the classroom may privately agree with this premise, but most students accept the notion that racism and sexism produce nothing but injustices which should not be tolerated. With respect to religion, though, most students and teachers are not operating from this basic understanding. In this sense, working with something like racism is different because we are, in a Socratic kind of way through a series of prompts and questions, leading students to the foregone conclusion that it helps no one. Religion does not offer such a clear-cut target for our mutual disapproval, as the variety of valuable and tolerable views rooted in religion is almost infinite. Hence the importance of developing viable approaches for productively working with this particular subject in the writing course.

As an example of the approach I propose, I look to my father-in-law and the coup in Chile on September 11, 1973. In 2006, I remember walking with my wife Sonia down Av. Manuel Montt in Providencia, one of the metropolitan communities that make up Santiago. We came to a busy street called 11 de septiembre, and I took the opportunity to speak without thinking. "That's a nice tribute," I said. "You guys named a street after 9–11." She knew what I meant, and with a grin, she replied, "No, mi gringito pelaito [my bald little gringo]. That was the day of the coup, in '73."

At the time, I was still putting together what had happened on their 9–11. In our first apartment, we could sometimes hear the fútbol games in Estadio Nacional, where Sonia's father, Don Hugo, was imprisoned and tortured during the coup—or, as they say, el golpe de 11 de septiembre. I have since become familiar with names like Salvador Allende, Victor Jara, and Augusto Pinochet. I have also become more familiar with names I already knew, like Henry Kissinger and Richard Nixon.

I have never had a long or detailed conversation with Don Hugo about his personal experience during that time, but I've learned quite a bit from Sonia and others. For the most part, religious belief prompted a great deal of good in response to the coup, good that Don Hugo saw first-hand. He has always been an atheist, but he often speaks kindly of the Catholic Church. He has seen what it can do.

And "what it can do" is where we can work with religious belief in the composition course. Instead of starting with the wrong verb by proclaiming what organized prophetic religion *is,* we look first to what it *does,* for all of us, in this world that we share. As what it does constantly changes, we avoid stagnant standoffs like the following: God Is Great/God Is Not Great; He's a Delusion/He's Our Only Hope; He's Eternal Love/He's a Constant Horror. In his critique of the banking concept of education, Paulo Freire says that too often our educational system suffers from "narration sickness"; that is, what happens in the classroom is usually a lecture *from* the teacher *to* the students, with no real dialogue, or reflection, or collective creation of meaning (52–58). That scene has largely been addressed in the field of composition and rhetoric, but how we deal with religion could still, in many cases, be described as suffering from this same kind of sickness, with each side telling us who and what He is.

As students think and write about religion, we can avoid these kinds of dead ends by adhering to the following principles:

- look to lived experience
- emphasize contingency over ontological claims
- point to action ("does") rather than stasis ("is")
- interrogate usefulness for enhancing happiness here on Earth
- highlight mediation as opposed to compromise
- encourage live options in place of dead ones

The 9–11 example I offered with my father-in-law illustrates a number of these principles. His view of religious belief has been determined not by what it is in some concrete way, but by what it "did" for him and for others at a particular time in his life. It also illustrates a way in which religious belief became valuable and useful (a live option for seeing the world) despite his own personal inclinations, a way that for him brought together and disarmed conflicting worldviews. In addition, the term 9–11 itself is an example of how meaning and truth are contingent and based on lived experience, as that term means something very different to, for instance, New Yorkers who lived through September 2001 and those who lived in Santiago through September 1973. Adopting a lens based on these principles provides writing teachers with a way to include religious belief as something to think and write about in the composition course, a way to work with an essay like Updike's "On Being a Self Forever" that I ran away from when I first started teaching.

CHAPTER 1

A "Simple" Question

A careful analysis of the teacher-
student relationship at any level,
inside or outside the school, reveals
its fundamentally *narrative* character.
… The contents, whether values or
empirical dimensions of reality, tend in
the process of being narrated to become
lifeless and petrified.
—Paulo Freire

I am ashamed to think how easily we capitulate
to badges and names…. If I know your sect, I
anticipate your argument.
—Ralph Waldo Emerson

"What does religion do?" That's the question that drives this book, a question that works to avoid the petrified and static narratives which Freire and Emerson refer to above. As Susanne Langer tells us, our understanding "of any datum, any experience, any subject, is determined by the nature of our questions" (4). A world view, from the center, the left, or the right, "is characterized more by the *formulation* of its problems than by its solution to them. Its answers establish an edifice of facts; but its questions make the frame in which its picture of facts is plotted. They make more than the frame; they give the angle of perspective, the palette, the style in which the picture is drawn" (4). For most of my own life, comfortable in the positions my parents had taken, I felt sure that I knew what religion was. But as this book goes on to argue, we can get a much fuller and more honest portrait of almost anything if we step away from what we're already convinced it *is*, choose another verb, and ask ourselves a question.

So, what does religion do? It is, of course, not such a simple question. By asking it, though, we move in the right direction. In "A Church

11

Mary Can Love," Nicholas Kristof provides an example. He describes how the Catholic Church has gone awry by excluding women from positions of power and prominence, positions they could actually hold about 2000 years ago. He writes that the Vatican is now grappling "with the consequences of a patriarchal premodern mind-set: scandal, cover-up and the clumsiest self-defense since Watergate." He adds, "That old boys' club in the Vatican became as self-absorbed as other old boys' clubs, like Lehman Brothers, with similar results" (WK11).

Like the United States, Chile has been caught up in the worldwide sexual abuse crisis engulfing the Catholic Church, with prominent priests being investigated in a number of communities across the country. But, as Kristof says, "There's another Catholic Church as well, one I admire intensely." He goes on to tell the stories of several nuns, priests, and Catholic organizations that work tirelessly and selflessly to help those who need it in some of the most difficult parts of the world. This Catholic Church, he says, is not the same as the other one, "the rigid all-male Vatican hierarchy that seems out of touch when it bans condoms even among married couples where one partner is H.I.V.-positive," a church "obsessed with dogma and rules and distracted from social justice" (WK11). Kristof ends by writing, "So when you read about the scandals, remember that the Vatican is not the same as the Catholic Church. Ordinary lepers, prostitutes and slum-dwellers may never see a cardinal, but they daily encounter a truly noble Catholic Church in the form of priests, nuns and lay workers toiling to make a difference" (WK11). This was the church that my father-in-law came across during Pinochet's horrific dictatorship.

Kristof's article embodies part of the pragmatic spirit I propose for the writing class because it's not focused on defending or condemning what it claims the church to be. Before arriving at any conclusions, it asks us to consider the practical consequences of what different representatives of the church actually do in the world. Kristof says the church he admires is the one connected with the daily realities, needs, and experiences of common people—the church whose deeds fit with what believers and non-believers alike might agree upon as good and useful in the world. In this regard, he aligns nicely with many American pragmatists who shaped so much of our philosophical and educational thinking in the 19th and 20th centuries.

So, again, the hard question, put simply. What does religion do? Some say that it rapes children and then hides the crime. Others say that it feeds, protects, loves, and educates children all over the world. Based on experience, both appear to be true. If, however, we begin our conversation about religious belief by first recognizing that such contradictory statements can be supported by real-world experience, we are in a better position to converse and write more effectively about this difficult topic.

Roberto and Margarita

My wife Sonia writes a couple of weekly columns for *La Tercera*, one of two major newspapers in Chile (it's a very long, but small country). As I was working on this book, she happened to write an article I found especially interesting with respect to the pragmatic approach I try to describe. The title of her article is "Las Estrategias de las Parejas para Resolver sus Conflictos" ("Strategies of Married Couples for Resolving Their Conflicts"). Part of it is based on a study by la Universidad del Desarrollo to discover the secrets of Chilean couples who have been happily together for some time. One such couple, Roberto and Margarita, caught my eye in particular. Roberto is an atheist and Margarita is a Catholic who likes to display Christian symbols throughout the house. The key to resolving this issue, writes my wife, was that they figured it essentially had no solution. They suspected that the only way "to solve" the problem would be to change the beliefs of one or the other; that is to say, change part of one's character or personality. As that was not possible, or desirable, they decided to concentrate on the common project, the common goal of their partnership. Instead of trying to fundamentally resolve the conflict, they worked to recognize it as part of who they were as a couple so they could move beyond it, or even use it as a source of strength (Lira 6).

This couple seemed to instinctively understand what years of research at the University of Washington has discovered—that even the happiest of marriages can only hope to "resolve" maybe thirty percent of their conflicts (6). What was especially interesting for me, however, was one of the ways in which couples like Roberto and Margarita were able to do what they did. One bad habit that Chilean couples have, apparently, is to criticize each other for *being* one thing or another. For example, instead of saying, "I don't like the way you leave your dirty clothes lying around," the wife might simply say, "you are so lazy" (7). The husband, then, tends to get defensive and responds with an accusation of his own, telling his wife what he truly believes her to be. The study finds, however, that couples who can frame their disagreements in terms of what the other one *does* rather than in terms of what the other one *is* have a much better chance for a healthy marriage (we're more likely to listen if it's certain behavior that comes under attack and not an essential part of our being). So rather than Margarita hearing that she was stupid for believing in God, or Roberto hearing that he was an unfeeling cynic, they worked to frame their criticisms in terms of what their faith, or lack thereof, pushed them to do. And then they went from there (7).

The Public Role of Religion: Some Preliminary Thoughts

We may do well in the writing class to remind our students that our public discourse about religion is shaped by our private beliefs, and vice versa. They don't exist in separate vacuums, but constantly inform one another in a cyclical kind of way. On election day, for instance, the public world is shaped by our private beliefs, and our private beliefs are continuously shaped by the public world in which we live—by family members, classmates, colleagues, the church, the government, the media, etc. Whether one would like to or not, in the U.S. there is little chance in the foreseeable future of "removing" religion from the public square in which we debate and decide public policy. For that to happen, it would have to be removed from private lives as well, a step some have argued is necessary for our collective survival (see, for example, *The End of Faith* by Sam Harris). As we saw with Roberto and Margarita, however, this is not a desirable option. And even if it were, it's not a viable one, given that polls consistently say about 90 percent of Americans hold some form of religious belief.

In the composition course, one thing we can do is require that ideas rooted in religion are held to the same standards as any other ideas that come up for debate with respect to public policy. Some argue that this is simply another way to give religious believers short shrift on the public stage. In *The Culture of Disbelief*, for example, Stephen Carter laments that "we often ask our citizens to split their public and private selves, telling them in effect that it is fine to be religious in private, but there is something askew when those private beliefs become the basis for public action" (Carter 8). There is, I agree, a problem when ideas based on religious belief are immediately discounted because of where they come from. They should be allowed to compete (a moot point, really, as they are already there, competing). But no idea should get a free pass; none should be allowed to power public action on the sole basis of their origin regardless of the impact they have on actual people or whether they are in tune with our other democratic principles.

To put it another way, we can look to a passage from Barack Obama's "'Call to Renewal' Keynote Address" in 2006. He writes,

> We all know the story of Abraham and Isaac. Abraham is ordered by God to offer up his only son, and without argument, he takes Isaac to the mountaintop, binds him to an altar, and raises his knife, prepared to act as God has commanded. Of course, in the end God sends down an angel to intercede at the very last moment, and Abraham passes God's test of devotion. But it's fair to say that if any of us leaving this church saw Abraham on a roof of a building raising his knife, we would, at the very least, call the police and expect the Department of Children and Family Services to take Isaac away from Abraham. We would do so because we do not hear what Abraham hears, do not see what Abraham sees, true as those experiences may be. So the best we can do is act in accordance with those things that we all see, and that we all hear, be it common laws or basic reason [5–6].

The Ten Commandments serve as another example. Some of them coincide with our other beliefs about how to construct a democratic society. Others do not, nor are they in "accordance with the things that we all see, and that we all hear."

Carter, however, says that asking a person to keep his or her religion a private matter trivializes that belief, and that we must fight against a culture that treats religion "like building model airplanes, just another hobby; something quiet, something private, something trivial" (22). In "Enacting Faith: Evangelical Discourse and the Discipline of Composition Studies," Lizbeth A. Rand begins by referring to Carter and pointing out that in the field of composition and rhetoric "our own discourse at times trivializes and misrepresents faith-related expression" (350). Rand's was an indispensable voice as our field began to turn its attention to religious belief, and her point about the discourse of many writing teachers regarding religion is well taken. But Carter's claim that to privatize faith necessarily leads to trivializing it is worth more attention. As Richard Rorty points out in his response to Carter's argument, "our family and love lives are private, nonpolitical and nontrivial. The poems we atheists write, like the prayers our religious friends raise, are private, nonpolitical, and nontrivial." There are, Rorty continues, "lots of other private pursuits that both give meaning to individual human lives and are such that mature, public-spirited adults are quite right in not attempting to use them as a basis for politics. The search for private perfection, pursued by theists and atheists alike, is neither trivial nor, in a pluralistic democracy, relevant to public policy" (*Philosophy* 170).

I think most would agree that our various pursuits for private perfection are by no means trivial, but some might question the notion that they are irrelevant to public policy. Our thoughts about the common good, it would seem, come primarily from our private worlds and our private beliefs. The point, though, is that it doesn't matter where the belief comes from; it only matters how useful that belief is to all of us. As a community, the individual *search* for private perfection is not our concern—we need only focus on the communal consequences of that search. A belief could come from a Batman comic, a walk in the woods, a hallucination, or the Bible. As Rorty suggests, again in response to Carter,

> The epistemology suitable for [our] democracy is one in which the only test of a political proposal is its ability to gain assent from people who retain radically diverse ideas about the point and meaning of human life, about the path to private perfection. The more such consensus becomes the test of a belief, the less important is the belief's source. So when Carter complains that religious citizens are forced "to restructure their arguments in purely secular terms before they can be presented," I should reply that "restructuring the arguments in purely secular terms" just means *dropping reference to the source of the premises of the arguments*, and that this omission seems a reasonable price to pay for religious liberty [173, emphasis mine].

This price Rorty refers to is, in fact, no more than any of us pay when proposing public policy. The test of a good idea is what it does in the world, not where it comes from.

In continuing to shift the focus away from a belief's origins and towards its consequences, Rorty outlines the term "anticlericalism." In "Anticlericalism and Atheism," he suggests that the argument over whether or not God really exists is beside the point, and therefore so too are the tags "theist" and "atheist." He describes himself as an anticleric rather than an atheist because "anticlericalism is a political view, not an epistemological or metaphysical one" (*Future* 33). In making his argument, Rorty refers to the thinking of Gianni Vattimo who, Rorty says, "wants to dissolve the problem of the coexistence of natural science with the legacy of Christianity by identifying Christ neither with truth nor with power but with love alone" (36). The direction that both Rorty and Vattimo pursue here aligns in many respects with John Dewey's distinction between "religion" as an institutional noun beholden to certain truths and "religious" as a contingent adjective beholden only to acts of love and human happiness (a distinction we pursue further, together with Charles Peirce's "Gospel of Greed" and "Gospel of Love").

Vattimo develops his argument from the idea of kenosis, whereby God relinquishes everything to us. This perspective, Vattimo writes, aims in part to pave "the way for a renewed dialogue with the Christian tradition, to which I have always belonged (as the rest of modernity), yet whose meaning has become incomprehensible to me" (*Future* 65). A new dialogue is desperately needed, he argues, if we are "to avoid the impasse in which modern consciousness always finds itself when confronted by Christian revelation: the impossibility of adhering to a doctrine that appears too sharply contrasted with the 'conquests' of enlightened reason, too full of myths which demand to be unmasked" (66). By exploring the meaning of kenosis—the transfer of love and charity from God to humans, or the act of incarnation—we can see that "Christ himself is the unmasker, and that the unmasking inaugurated by him ... is the meaning of the history of salvation itself" (66). Within this process of unmasking—a process in which we take an active role by continuing what Christ started—Vattimo urges that

> [Believing] in salvation will not mean adhering to the letter of every-
> thing that is written in the Gospel and in the dogmatic teaching of the

Church, but rather in trying to understand the meaning of the evangelical text for me, here, now. In other words, reading the signs of the times with no other provision than the commandment of love [66].

As the search for meaning has been handed over to us and that search is necessarily contingent, faith is no longer about foundational truth and power, but rather situational love and charity, or contextual responsibility to other human beings (treating each other as equals). In this light, we can see "all the great unmaskers of the West, from Copernicus and Newton to Darwin, Nietzsche, and Freud, as carrying out works of love" (*Future* 38). They were, as Vattimo puts it, "reading the signs of the times" with the goal of increasing the possibility for human happiness. From this perspective, people like Freud, Darwin, and Marx may be understood as leading religious figures, continuing Christ's work.

Karl Marx, for example, has been widely misunderstood when it comes to religious belief. "The classical Marxist critique of religion," as Cornel West notes, "is not an a priori philosophical rejection of religion; rather, it is a social analysis of and historical judgment upon religious practices" (*Reader* 373). In fact, "contrary to such widespread crypto–Marxist myths about religion, Marx and Engels understood religion as a profound human response to, and protest against, intolerable conditions" (373). For both Marx and Engels, religious belief had the possibility of being intimately bound up with Vattimo's point that "being is event, a recognition that enables me to enter actively into history, instead of passively contemplating its necessary laws.... [T]his is the meaning of the statement 'I no longer call you servants but friends'" (*Belief* 78).

If we can get our students in the habit of blurring those stark dividing lines between figures like Christ and Darwin, we'll have a better chance at working with this difficult topic in the writing class.

A Bad Reputation

The pragmatists are often misunderstood, often seen as relativists who simply go by another name. In his defense of Truth—that is, objectively verifiable truth—Felipe Fernandez-Armesto writes that "some of the most dedicated enemies of truth call themselves pragmatists," and that pragmatism, specifically in the hands of Richard Rorty, is nothing more than "relativism in disguise" (181, 220). More recently, in his book *The End of Faith: Religion, Terror, and the Future of Reason* (a book that was on and off the *New York Times* best-seller list for over a year), Sam Harris takes this same misguided position. He claims that "if we ever hope to reach a global consensus on matters of ethics—if we would say, for instance, that stoning women for adultery is *really* wrong, in some absolute sense—we must find deep reasons to reject pragmatism" (179). To support this claim, Harris argues that the pragmatic method holds that "to call a statement 'true' is merely to praise it for how it functions in some area of discourse; it is not to say anything about how it relates to the universe at large" (179). He says that there are, in fact, general truths to be known about the way the world is, and to suggest (as he sees the pragmatists suggesting) that you can't ever be "right" about anything—that one should only focus on the usefulness of a belief in a particular context—will inevitably lead to trouble. He offers the following example: "If a literalist reading of the Bible works for you on Sundays, while agnosticism about God is better suited to Mondays at the office, there is no reason to worry about the resulting contradictions in your worldview" (180).

Whether Harris is referring to neo-pragmatists like Richard Rorty who focus more on language or pragmatists like Peirce, James, and Dewey who pay more attention to action, he misses a central point: both schools of thought are concerned with confronting the contradictions in our beliefs. While Harris is right about their rejection of resounding universal truths, he fails to recognize that the principal aim of these pragmatists is to examine the tangible consequences of our beliefs so we can critique/reconcile those beliefs and enhance human happiness. This approach is grounded in a responsibility to people, not to finding an ultimate Truth. Times change. People change. To say something will remain True for all time doesn't allow for such change, nor does it often allow for an honest view of lived experience. A pragmatist would begin by asking something like this: "What difference would it practically make to anyone if this notion rather than that notion were true?" (James, *Pragmatism* 23). That is, "the pragmatic method ... is to try to interpret each notion by tracing its respective practical consequences" (23).

In addition, we need to "square" our notions with all of our other notions. It's a system of checks and balances based on our experience in the world. To take, for instance, Harris' example of shifting from a literal interpretation of the Bible on Sunday to a more agnostic approach on Monday, a pragmatist would argue that it's our duty to examine the practical consequences of doing so and then work to reconcile the underlying beliefs. In other words, each belief is only as good as our other beliefs allow. As James writes, "If theological ideas prove to have value for concrete life, they will be true for pragmatism, in the sense of being good for so much. For how much more they are true, [that] will depend entirely on their relations to the other truths that also have to be acknowledged" (*Pragmatism* 35). So with respect to stoning women for adultery, a pragmatist would come to the same conclusion as Harris—that this is wrong and we shouldn't do it—but by a better method: a method that ensures we don't get bogged down in any antiquated truths that can never be challenged.

Richard Rorty, I think, offers a good example here. Referring to Albrecht Wellmer, Rorty says, "We agree that one reason to prefer democracies is that they enable us to construct ever bigger and better contexts of discussion. But I stop there, and Wellmer goes on. He adds that this reason is not just a justification of democracy *for us*, but 'a justification, *period*'" (*Rorty and His Critics* 13). Rorty suggests that for a pragmatist, it's crucial to make the distinction between "whether I think of my scalpel or my computer as 'a good tool for this task' or as a 'good tool, *period*'" (13). He goes on to say that "our responsibility to Truth, or to Reason, must be replaced by talk about our responsibility to our fellow human beings" (*Social Hope* 148). We do not have a "responsibility to get things right. Rather, it is a responsibility to ourselves to make our beliefs cohere with one another, and to our fellow humans to make them cohere with theirs" (149). It's an approach that has everything to do with worrying about contradictions in how we see the world, and how the world sees us—an ongoing task of engaging in conversations that work toward reconciling our own beliefs and understandings with those who disagree with us.

Emerson and Beecher: Some Central Roots

The pragmatists I discuss in this book build in many ways on the work of Ralph Waldo Emerson. His influence on the pragmatic thinking that helped to shape this country is almost boundless. As one example, I point to a chapter titled "Religion" from his book *English Traits* in which he makes the following comparison: "It is with religion as with marriage. A youth marries in haste; afterwards, when his mind is opened to the reason of the conduct of life, he is asked what he thinks of the institution of marriage and of the right relations of the sexes. 'I should have much to say,' he might reply, 'if the question were open, but I have a wife and children, and all question is closed for me'" (503). He reminds us that all too often we resign ourselves early on to the way in which we assume things have to be, and in doing so completely ignore our own real-world experiences which might, if examined, prompt us to ask some interesting questions. With respect to religious dogma that is so often passed from one generation to another, Emerson observes that it's so much easier to more or less concede, and "find some niche or crevice in this mountain of stone which religious ages have quarried and carved, wherein to bestow yourself, than attempt anything ridiculously and dangerously above your strength, like removing it" (504). We have to act of our own initiative, he says, to fully realize that religion is alive, breathing and shouting and whispering in so many different ways. "Where dwells religion?" he asks. "Tell me first where dwells electricity, or motion, or thought, or gesture. They do not dwell or stay at all." Like electricity, Emerson suggests that religion is "passing, glancing, gesticular; it is a traveler, a newness, a surprise, a secret" (513). As such, it cannot be confined into any particular compartment.

At the same time that Emerson was writing, Henry Ward Beecher was offering similar advice. Beecher has been called "America's most prominent nineteenth-century liberal preacher and [...] perhaps the most powerful preacher in American history, if not in the history of the Anglo-Saxon people" (Chandler 19). People like Abraham Lincoln and Walt Whitman, as well as Emerson and nearly all of the luminaries of their day (including, of course, Beecher's famous sister) sat in his church at one time or another. He was, to put it crudely, a rock star.

An essential aspect of Beecher's faith was his attempt to harmonize spirituality with the "real world"; he worked to dispel the assumed conflict between theological tenets and secular truths. As William McLoughlin tells us, "Beecher's great achievement was to amalgamate Romanticism, religion, and science—the epistemology of Kant, the

Gospel of Jesus, the teleology of Spencer" (4). He preached "to the throbbing human heart, to reaffirm its faith in Christianity, and yet to do so without undermining the equally profound faith of Americans in science, education, and learning—in short, to harmonize religion and science not through metaphysical speculation ... but through appealing to emotional experience" (39). Beecher writes in a letter to Theodore Tilton, "I discern, arising in studies in Natural Science, a surer foothold for these [evangelical] views than they have ever had. Insofar as theology is concerned, if I have one purpose or aim, it is to secure for the truths now developing in the sphere of Natural Science a religious spirit and harmonization with all the cardinal truths of religion" (McLoughlin Prepreface). Referring to two classical pillars of Western philosophy, Beecher offers the following harmony: "It has been said that everybody is either a Platonist or an Aristotelian—Plato standing for ideal philosophy and Aristotle for the real and practical. Everybody tends, it is said, to follow one or the other. No; the perfect man unites them both, and is at once Aristotelian and Platonist. His feet standing on solid fact, his head goes philosophizing, and his heart keeps the balance between them" (Howard, John R. 158).

As with Emerson, Beecher's work not only illustrates his ongoing attempt to square secular and spiritual truths, it advocates an activity that fights against the static aspect of dogma. Emerson writes,

> The sacredness which attaches to the act of creation, the act of thought, is transferred to the record. The poet chanting is felt to be a divine man: henceforth the chant is divine also. The writer was a just and wise spirit: henceforth it is settled the book is perfect; as love of the hero corrupts into worship of his statue. Instantly the book becomes noxious: the guide is a tyrant [55].

Pushing this point, Emerson adds, "Books are for the scholar's idle times. When he can read God directly, the hour is too precious to be wasted in other men's transcripts of their readings" (57): "The one thing in the world, of value, is the active soul" (56). This focus on activity, on the notion that real and useful knowledge generally comes from lived experience—"Only so much do I know, as I have lived" (59)—prompts us to understand that new experiences will inevitably challenge existing beliefs. Our beliefs, our habits, our truths must constantly change as our experiences tell us something doesn't work anymore. On this note,

Beecher suggests that too many people are alarmed "at the inevitable changes in theology and government and the conditions of the people. They want peace. Well, you can find it in the graveyard, and that is the only place. Among living men you can find no peace. Growth means disturbance; peace in any such sense as that of no investigation, no change, means death" (*Lectures* 126).

Just as Emerson did, Beecher offered this advice over and over: "There must be, in any healthful society, a process of absorption, or of reconstruction of its organizations.... A society whose institutions are unchanging is itself ungrowing. The living body alters. Only the dead rest" (*Life Thoughts* 62). Taking the specific example of prayer, he writes, "Do not come to me and tell me you are fit to join the church because you love to pray morning and night. Tell me what your praying has *done* for you; and then call your neighbors, and let me hear what they think it has done for you" (*Life Thoughts* 121). The simple habit of praying and the unreflective belief that it is worthwhile are inconsequential. Like all else, the value of prayer should be judged—here, by us—based on what it does in the world, just as the value of religion may be assessed in the writing course.

A French Connection

In "American Scholar" and elsewhere, Emerson tells us not to look over our shoulders at where we'd come from but to look at the new world in front of us for our thoughts and ideas on how to live. Good advice in so many ways, but new thinking, as Emerson also said, is rarely unconnected to ideas somewhere behind us or off to the side. Michel de Montaigne had a significant influence on not only Emerson but the rest of the Western world, as he has been called the father of the modern essay and perhaps of modernism itself. That blueprint for the personal essay that he gave to the world changed the way we see ourselves in part by validating our personhood and allowing us to accept our unique ideas and reactions to the world as valuable subjects for study, writing, and discourse.

With respect to religion, Montaigne was most closely aligned with Fideism, a theological bend that held we could only know God through faith and not through our ability to reason. Like most people living in his time, he made public statements acknowledging the rights and power of the Church. His essays, however, say very little on metaphysical Christian tenets and dogma. While he took ideas from religious and secular thinkers alike, he relied primarily on lived experience to formulate his conclusions—conclusions that usually ended with a statement like, "but then again, I'm not really sure."

Montaigne found most "professional" philosophers to be pretentious and not very useful, but he was drawn to the Hellenistic thinking put forth by the Stoics, Skeptics, and Epicureans from around the third century BC. As Sarah Bakewell writes, he was fascinated with these "great pragmatic schools which explored such questions as how to cope with a friend's death, how to act well in morally difficult situations, and how to make the most of life" (109). A focus on moderation, gaining control of one's emotions, and living in the present were central themes for these thinkers, and evident in Montaigne's own writing. He also emphasized that nothing is static or certain: "We, and our judgment, and all mortal things go on flowing and rolling unceasingly ... both the judging and the judged being in continual change and motion" (130). We must work hard to get in the habit, he said, of understanding that we might actually be wrong. "No propositions astonish me," he writes, and "no belief offends me, whatever contrast it offers with my own" (170). Bakewell adds that Montaigne "liked being contradicted, as it opened up more interesting conversations and helped him to think." (170).

Having lived through the horrors of Catholic and Protestant fighting that included the St. Bartholomew's Day massacres, Montaigne insisted that such a perspective would improve our collective lot in the world. The characteristic conclusions—"I suspend judgment," or "Then again, I'm not so sure"—that he drew in many of his essays were in large part aimed at fostering an open mind to effect change on the ground, so to speak. The ability to leave one's own shoes, however, and occupy another's does not come easily to most; it's something we need to force ourselves to do, and it is the driving force behind many of his essays, including "On Cruelty." Once we get in the habit of taking this perspective, though (as habit, he felt, dictates most of what we do), it starts to come naturally.

We can find a similar strain in the thinking of Marcel Proust who, like his compatriot Montaigne, brought to the fore the value of routine lived experience, such as the taste of a madeleine drenched in tea. Proust, writing at about the same time as John Dewey in the 19th and 20th century, drew a distinction between spirituality and the belief in an omniscient and omnipotent God. A strong believer in the former and curious about the latter, Proust's extraordinary novel *Remembrance of Things Past* is full of metaphysical musings and idealistic interpretations.

God does not appear in much of his writing, but He is not by any means missing. "If I have no religion," Proust writes in a letter, "on the other hand a religious preoccupation has never been absent for a single day from my life" (White 34–5). Perhaps, he submits, there is a heaven, or an afterlife, in which we will meet again as our individual selves in a better place. But "the more one is religious," he notes,

> the less one dares to move towards certainty…; I don't deny anything, I believe in the possibility of everything, while objections based on the existence of Evil, etc. strike me as absurd, since Suffering alone seems to me to have made (and to continue to make) Man a bit more than a brute. But to go from that on to certainty, even to Hope, is a long journey. I haven't yet crossed that threshold—will I ever? [35].

Proust touches here on common and reasonable claims both for and against the Christian proposition (the existence of evil as proof that God does not exist, and the existence of suffering as proof that He does). In the next chapter we come back to such intellectual claims regarding the essence of God, none of which, as Dewey suggests, should be entertained—and none of which, I argue, should be entertained in the composition class. In addition, Proust's point that anything is possible is a powerful pragmatic element—one we explore at length with William James. His reference to a "long journey" and to wondering about ever crossing a threshold suggests another central pragmatic theme, that beliefs and truths be continuously supported by hard-earned, lived experience.

His emphasis on life experience corresponds with the way in which Proust put far "more faith in the senses and in memory than in the intellect" when it came to drawing conclusions about the world around us (35). Memory, of course, plays an indispensable role in *Remembrance*, specifically those involuntary memories that splash upon us unexpectedly when we hear or smell or see something that triggers them. As Edmund White puts it, the "idea of involuntary memory would become one of the touchstones of *Remembrance of Things Past* and one of his chief principles of literary architecture" (42). And involuntary memory, of course, is by no means rooted in certainty.

Agee's A Death in the Family: *An Extended Example*

Possibility, fallibility, and the importance of lived experience, all found in the writings of Montaigne and Proust, are crucial when considering the question, "What does religion do?" James Agee's celebrated novel provides a more contemporary (and distinctly American) illustration of answering that question, and as opposing views of religious belief are so eloquently wrought and easily recognizable for first-year writing students, it's worth discussing in some detail. From the beginning, the marriage of Jay and Mary is divided by the Christian faith: she believes, and he does not. Mary was beginning to realize the weight of "their religious difference, or the importance of the difference to her" (46). She was not sure how important this difference was to him, but it was clear that when it came to religion both of them "said so very little, as if both took care to say very little. [And] that was just it. That a thing which meant so much to her, so much more, all the time, should be a thing that they could not share, or could not be open about" (46). The characters who surround Mary run the spectrum of believers and nonbelievers, including her aunt Hannah who shares her faith and her husband Jay who she was convinced "felt none of [her brother] Andrew's anger and contempt, and none of her father's irony, but it was clear by his special quietness, when instances of it came up, that he was very far away from it, and from her" (46). Mary was determined, though, to raise good Catholic children, and to make sure "that the family remain one, that the gulf be closed" (46).

With Jay's untimely death, however, she doesn't get a chance to meet that particular challenge. We see, though, how her religion has affected her relationship with other members of her family, including her father, Joel, who thinks "the real estrangement ... was the whole stinking morass of churchiness that really separated them, and now that was apt to get worse rather than better" (110). Her father is fond of quoting Shakespeare, like when he says to her, right after Jay's death, it's "just the way things go. As flies to wanton boys. That's all." Mary replies "No.... No, Papa. It's not that way," and her father says to himself, "If she tries to tell me it's God's inscrutable mercy, I'll have to leave the room" (131).

As the principal characters sit in Mary's living room, coping with the news of Jay's accident, we are treated to an extraordinary view of a common exchange when it comes to religion. Everyone, except for Joel, feels a presence in the house, a presence understood to be Jay's spirit. Even Catherine, Mary's mostly deaf mother, senses something. Joel, however, remains unconvinced. "All the same," he says, "it can't be what you think." Mary responds,

> "I don't know what it was, Papa, but there are four of us here independently who are sure it was something."
> "Joel, I know that God in a wheelbarrow wouldn't convince you," his sister [Hannah] said. "We aren't even trying to convince you. But while you're being so rational, why at least please be rational enough to realize that we experienced what we experienced."
> "The least I can do is accept the fact that three people had a hallucination, and honor their belief in it.... I believe you, for yourself, Hannah. All of you. I'd have to have the same hallucination myself to be convinced. And even then I'd have my doubts."
> "What on earth do you mean *doubts*, Papa, if you had it yourself?"
> "I'd suspect it was just a hallucination."
> "Oh, good Lord! You've got it going and coming, haven't you!"
> "'Is this a dagger that I see before me?' Wasn't, you know. But you could never convince Macbeth it wasn't" [144].

The book, overall, treats the topic of religious belief as if wrestling with an octopus, questioning faith and common sense alike. The novel ends on this topic—it ends on the edge of the coin, so to speak, as if tipping its hat to both sides. At the funeral Andrew sees a "perfectly magnificent butterfly" settle on the coffin, "right over the breast ... just barely making his wings breathe, like a heart" (251). In beautiful detail, Andrew later describes to Rufus (Jay and Mary's little boy) the descent of this butterfly to the bottom of the grave, atop the coffin, and then its majestic ascent up into the heavens. Trying to make sense of what he saw, Andrew says to Rufus, "If there are any such things as miracles, then *that's* surely miraculous" (252).

At the very same time, Andrew is also incensed at the Reverend Jackson and the church because they said that Jay could not receive a full burial service as he had never been baptized. His wonder at the butterfly and his rage at the Reverend are both, in almost the same breath, unloaded upon young Rufus. "Priggish, mealy-mouthed son of a bitch," Andrew says. "And they call themselves Christians." For all the "ducking and bowing and scraping, and basting themselves with the signs of the Cross, and all that disgusting hocus-pocus, and you come to one simple, single act of Christian charity and what happens? The rules of the Church forbid it. He's not a member of our little club" (253).

On the last page of the novel, Rufus tries to make sense of it all. One moment, his uncle talked with such love and passion, even talked about believing in God, and the next, he spoke with such hatred in his eyes that Rufus got scared. Rufus starts to sense that this hatred was aimed not just at the Reverend Jackson and the church, but also at his mother and Aunt Hannah. But how, he wonders, can his uncle hate his own family? "He loves them. But how can he love them if he hates them so? How can he hate them if he loves them?" (254). These questions, asked by a child, are the same kinds of questions that come up in the middle of the book, when Mary and Hannah are talking about Jay. Mary is wondering if her father ever really liked Jay: "but what *am* I to make of it?" she asks. There he was, "praising Jay to the skies on the one hand, and on the other, why practically in the same breath, telling me one reason after another why it would be plain foolhardiness to marry him. What would *you* think?"

> "Can't you see that both things might be so—or that he might very sincerely have felt that both things were so, rather?"
>
> Mary thought for a moment. "I don't know, Aunt Hannah. No, I don't see quite how."
>
> "You learned how yourself, Mary."
>
> "Did I!"
>
> "You learned there was a lot in what your father—in all our misgivings, but learning it never changed your essential opinion of him, did it? You found you could realize both things at once."
>
> "That's true. Yes. I did."
>
> "We had to learn more and more that was good. You had to learn more and more that wasn't so good" [101].

For our purposes in the composition course, we can take these last lines by Hannah to heart. By looking at what religious belief does in the world,

28

those of us who need to may see more of the good while others who need to may see more of the bad. As a result, we can prompt students to "realize both things at once," both the good and the bad, without aiming to change their "essential opinions" on the existence of God. Agee's novel, in fact, illustrates a number of themes developed by pragmatists that can help us write about religion, such as looking to lived experience, struggling to acknowledge and square those different experiences, and distinguishing between a dogmatic institution of religion and religious sensibilities found in all walks of life.

CHAPTER 2

Happy Harmonizing: Peirce, James, and Dewey on Religion

Whatever inspiration is, it's born from a continuous
"I Don't Know...." Knowledge that doesn't lead to
new questions quickly dies out. It fails to maintain the
temperature required for sustaining life.
—Wislawa Szymborska

Let us, on both sides, lay aside all arrogance.
Let us not, on either side, claim that we have
already discovered the truth. Let us seek it
together as something which is known to
neither of us.
—St. Augustine

The signal, if implicit, motive of Pragmatism
is the realization of thinking as a life form,
subject to the same processes of growth and
change as all other life forms.
—Joan Richardson

In this chapter I focus on Charles Sanders Peirce, William James, and John Dewey not only because they were principal authors of American pragmatism, but because they were preoccupied with education (especially James and Dewey) as well as religion. For the most part, the prominent philosophies that helped to shape nineteenth- and twentieth-century European thought deemphasized the value of religious belief. Such was not the case, however, in America. As Cornel West writes, "Religious concerns loomed large in the first significant American philosophical response to modernity. The first generation of American Pragmatists, especially Charles Peirce and William James, attempted not only to demythologize modern science, but also to update religion." In fact, West adds that "nowhere in the modern world did philosophers take religion more seriously than in the United States between 1900 and 1940" (*Reader* 361).

As a scientist and one of America's most influential philosophers, Peirce wrote extensively on religion, including essays like "Evolutionary Love" and "The Concept of God," in which he often placed a premium on faith by suggesting that we rely more in life on vague intuitions than on the precision of reason. In the work of James, understood by many as the greatest psychologist of his day, we find essays like "The Will to Believe" and books such as *Talks to Teachers* and *The Varieties of Religious Experience*. As Bennett Ramsey argues, "The nature of James' work overall ... finds its whither and its whence in a developing understanding and an increasingly strong avowal of the human person as a religiously bounded self" (3). In the philosophy of John Dewey, who for the better part of a century transformed our understanding of the education process, we find books like *A Common Faith*, in which he explores religion with the goal of increasing its potential for improving our lives. In short, these educators took religion seriously, and their insights can prove invaluable for us today, both in and out of the writing class.

Charles Sanders Peirce: It Is What It Does

Charles Sanders Peirce was a scientist, a mathematician, and a logician, but his pragmatic perspective of the world consisted of far more than facts and figures. Peirce thought science and religion could and should work together, with the common goal of improving our lives on this planet. He took issue with several prominent scientific and positivistic movements of his time, and he worked to refute their claims of "infallible certainty" so as to "keep open the possibility of discovering a rational reconciliation of science with religious values as expressions of human needs" (*Charles* 345). His attempt at this reconciliation, with its emphasis on action and human experience in a social setting, propelled the pragmatic approach that inspired William James, John Dewey, Richard Rorty, Cornel West, and others. As West puts it, "Peirce's double consciousness of experimental inquiry and common human sentiments

31

and his dual allegiance to scientific method and Christian faith serve as the soil upon which the seeds of American Pragmatism sprout" (*Evasion* 49).

It is first important to clarify how Peirce defines science and religion and how such a mindset can be useful to the thinking and writing of composition students in the twenty-first century. In an especially appropriate essay called "The Marriage of Religion and Science," he asks the most basic question, "What is science?" He answers,

> The Dictionary will say that it is systematized knowledge.... Mere knowledge [however], though it be systematized, may be a dead memory; while by science we all habitually mean a living and growing body of truth.... That which constitutes science, then, is not so much correct conclusions, as it is a correct method. But the method of science is itself a scientific result. It did not spring out of the brain of a beginner: it was a historic attainment and a scientific achievement.... That which is essential, however, is the scientific spirit, which is determined not to rest satisfied with existing opinions [*Charles* 350].

He also asks "What is religion?" and suggests that

> In each individual it is a sort of sentiment, or obscure perception, a deep recognition of a something in the circumambient All which, if he strives to express it, will clothe itself in forms more or less extravagant, more or less accidental, but ever acknowledging the first and last ... as well as a relation to that Absolute of the individual's self, as a relative being [351].

Religion and science, then, for Peirce the American Pragmatist, are quite properly compatible. For him, they each involve a method that moves beyond a focus on the individual and that is ever open to change. Today, in the early twenty-first century, we seem to find little that is compatible between religion and science, and little that could be described by the idealistic title of Peirce's essay, "The Marriage of Religion and Science." Our country's ongoing court battles over the inclusion of religious beliefs in public school curriculum (the latest of which in Ohio can be found in Circleville where Ohio Christian University "teaches 'biblical truth' to public high school students" [Biliczky]) as well as recent U.S. Supreme Court decisions like *Town of Greece v. Galloway* and *Burwell v. Hobby Lobby* (which tend to ignite angry and oppositional stances regarding religious expression in the public sphere) work to widen the gulf. A perspective such as Peirce's, that begins by seeing two different but compatible subjects, can guide us in the writing class.

One point of friction that Peirce explores is the way in which science pushes ahead while religion—as we try to express it and place ourselves in relation to it—tends to look to the past. As science constantly changes by growing and building upon itself, religion, Peirce says, is more "like a plucked flower, [and] its destiny is to wilt and fade" (351). What initially spawned religious sentiment "loses gradually its pristine purity and strength, till some new creed treads it down" (351). Such vivid language may easily seem to be advancing an impassioned campaign *against* religion; on the contrary, Peirce aims to bolster religion by insisting that *both* religion and science should be "animated by a progressive spirit" (352), and he offers his theory of agapism as one way to reconcile the two. Agapism, derived from the early Christian concept of *agape,* the perfect spiritual love that transcends the physical, can appeal to the imaginations of modern college students, whether theists or not. Peirce, in fact, intended his own iteration of agapism as a response to Darwin's *Origin of the Species.* He takes the ancient ideal of *agape,* or pure love, and factors in both chance and the blind mechanics of natural selection. And of these three—natural selection, chance, and love—he sees love as the primary force. Peirce admits that his proposal "will probably shock my scientific brethren" (*Philosophy* 364), but he is adamant in arguing that understanding who we are and how we came to be this way cannot be accomplished by chance and science alone. For a scientist, he braves the waters of spiritualism and emotion, or what he calls "feeling": "if it were possible to believe in agapism without believing it warmly, that fact would be an argument against the truth of the doctrine. At any rate, since the warmth of feeling exists, it should on every account be candidly confessed" (364).

At the heart of what drives his argument here lies a rejection of the Cartesian focus on the inner self and, in its place, an emphasis on our social web as having powered our evolution. For example, Peirce refers to St. John and the idea "that growth comes only from love, from—I will not say self-*sacrifice,* but from the ardent impulse to fulfill another's highest impulse" (362). There is a focus on being responsible to other people, a responsibility that is alive and in the present. Such a pragmatic approach to religion that Peirce offers can be attractive to those of us in the writing course because it de-mythologizes religion and transforms it into something practical and relevant. To this same end, Peirce also tried to turn "the scientific method into a human affair, [or] a set of distinct social practices by which knowledge is produced." Ultimately, his pragmatism as a "cultural demystifying activity ... permits Peirce to defend religion, not devalue or dismiss it" (West, *Evasion* 43–44).

Peirce was a practicing scientist for twenty years, but he could not accept what he saw as the Darwinian dismissal of the human spirit. In "Evolutionary Love," he writes that as "Darwin puts it on his title page, it is the struggle for existence; and he should have added for his motto: every individual for himself, and the Devil take the hindmost!" (*Philosophy* 364). He puts Darwin's theory of evolution in a layman's religious terms:

> Here, then is the issue. The Gospel of Christ says that progress comes from every individual merging his individuality in sympathy with his neighbors. On the other side, the conviction of the nineteenth century is that progress takes place by virtue of every individual's striving for himself with all his might and trampling his neighbor underfoot whenever he gets a chance to do so. This may accurately be called the Gospel of Greed [364].

Needless to say, the late twentieth and early twenty-first centuries have also seen their share of the "Gospel of Greed." It is a phenomenon that some of our students may be very willing to applaud ("Greed is Good," as Gordon Gekko says in the movie *Wall Street*), but most seem to reject it. And they reject it for ethical, moral reasons that usually grow directly from the various religious teachings many of them have learned from early childhood. Such a pragmatic perspective that Peirce advances can thus be highly valuable in a composition course that encourages students to consider the question, "What can religion do?"

In advocating for a Gospel of Love based on social responsibility instead of the Gospel of Greed, Peirce appeals to what he calls the "Sensible Heart" with the church playing an indispensable role as social catalyst. Again, this concept of living one's life by the rules of social responsibility can resonate in the minds of students who draw from various religious traditions when it comes to human ethical conduct. He suggests that without a very public, vibrant, national church, our evolution as civilized beings would be difficult. Further, he argues that "religion is a great, perhaps the greatest, factor of that social life which extends beyond one's own circle of personal friends." To him, "that life is everything for elevated, and humane, and democratic civilization" (*Collected Papers* 6:449). Students should be encouraged to take such advice from a scientist seriously and turn to personal experiences and to readings from other courses that they are taking to explore examples of how religion shapes behavior.

In his essay "What is Christian Faith?" Peirce advises that "Man's highest developments are social" and that any religion can reach its ideal state only through the "bond of a common love of God accomplished by each man's loving his neighbor" (*Charles* 355). Such an ideal state, for Peirce, is the practical result of *agape,* or agapism, discussed above. He believed that a church could provide a way for individuals to connect with others, and he chastised those religious leaders who would segregate or even shun non-conformists: "who are you, anyway, who are so zealous to keep the churches small and exclusive?" (*Philosophy* 357). He added that "if one renounces the church, in what other way can one as satisfactorily exercise the faculty of fraternizing with all one's neighbors?" (*Collected Papers* 6:449).

One can imagine different responses to that rhetorical question, but Peirce's focus on the social, tangible consequences regarding the role of the church provides a path we can follow in a composition course. He tries to assuage the perceived conflict between religion and science by examining the consequences of our beliefs, a tact that he realized may appear to be "a skeptical and materialistic principle" but pointed out that "it is only an application of the sole principle of logic which was recommended by Jesus: 'Ye may know them by their fruits'" (*Collected Papers* 5:402).

In a vein appropriate for the composition course, Peirce stresses the social aspect of this principle by reminding us that the fruit is "collective, it is the achievement of the whole people" (5:402). He was adamant that our advance through time has been possible only through collective action and that no single individual has ever accomplished anything alone, including Darwin: "I doubt if any of the great discoveries ought, properly, to be considered as altogether individual achievements" (*Philosophy* 374). Thus, "religion cannot reside in its totality in a single individual. Like every species of reality, it is essentially a social, a public affair" (*Charles* 351). Within such a broader social context, composition students can, and do, examine and write about the social bonds that religion provides in their own worlds. It is an aspect of religion that is not competitive or argumentative in the spirit of "proving" one religion superior to others or in the spirit of vanquishing the errors of "false" prophets and their competing beliefs. It focuses on the business of what religion can do.

On the surface, this may appear to depart from Emerson's familiar focus on the individual and self-reliance, but Emerson too saw the individual as deeply connected to community. He writes in his essay, "History," that "there is really only one mind common to all men" in that most of us share similar perceptions of the world around us—or else we could not even communicate. For Emerson, only our particular place in history makes us unique. There is no pure originality; we quote everything; we are all interconnected. As he says at the outset of this essay, "I am the owner of Caesar's hand / and Plato's brain / of Lord Christ's heart / and Shakespeare's strain" (115). Peirce's amalgamation of science and religion was very much based on such an understanding of the individual within the larger community.

So too did Peirce draw on Emerson's thoughts about personal experience. While we are all interconnected and must in many ways rely on the past, it's essential to highlight our own everyday experiences in order to form and improve our beliefs. For Emerson, one must "explore and sit at the feet of the familiar, the low" and understand that "life [not the library] is our dictionary" (69, 61). And for Peirce, "the scientific spirit requires a man to be at all times ready to dump his whole cartload of beliefs, the moment experience is against them. The desire to learn forbids him to be perfectly cocksure that he knows already. Besides, positive science can only rest on experience; and experience can never result in absolute certainty" (*Collected Papers* 1:55). And rather than finding the "scientific spirit" diametrically opposed to the "religious spirit," Peirce finds that they rest their quests for truth upon the same foundation of individual experience: "It is easy to chop logic about matters of which you have no experience whatever.... A man may be an accomplished theologian without ever having felt the stirring of the spirit; but he cannot answer the simple question ['What is Christian Faith?'] except out of his own religious experience" (*Charles* 353).

Peirce placed a premium on lived experience for both faith and science, proposing that one can only grow "by experience continually pouring upon him ideas he has not yet acquired" (*Collected Papers* 5:402). And as Emerson insisted, these ideas could not just come only from others: "I appeal," Peirce writes, "to the typical Christian to answer out of the abundance of his spirit, without dictation from priests" (*Charles* 354). For, as he asks rhetorically in "The Concept of God," "where would such an idea, say as that of God, come from if not from direct experience?" (*Philosophy* 377). Such an approach fits well into composition classes where students are asked to weave together outside authority and their own lived experience into an original argument. One cautionary challenge—and opportunity—here is to help students negotiate the tension between the proselytization of a creed or dogma and the analysis of life experience.

With a similar note of caution, Peirce warns against what he calls "precision." He reminds his readers that "'God' is a vernacular word," and like every other vernacular word—indeed, more than most—it is extraordinarily "*vague*" (375). He is right, of course, in such a basic but often overlooked observation. The idea of "God" is an overwhelmingly powerful one that, for a believer, defines everything in that individual's experience. But although it is a concept that may be all-defining, it does not lend itself to specific definition. Thus, Peirce believed in the reality of God, but he believed just as strongly that one of the greatest errors we make concerning this reality is that we render Him too precise. "*No* concept, not even those of mathematics, is absolutely precise; and some of the most important for everyday use are extremely vague" (376). As Kenneth Burke later called "rotten with perfection" (a term which describes our innate desire to establish perfect definitions and then cling to them), Peirce saw much of humanity's troubles with religion as rooted in our common inability to accept uncertainty—hence our wrongheaded pursuit of absolute truths. "Those who are given to defining too much," he says, "inevitably run themselves into confusion" (376).

Vague instinct and ambiguity occupy a privileged place for Peirce when it comes to both religion and science. "[W]e all think," he writes, "that there is an element of order in the universe. Could any laboratory experiments render that proposition more certain than instinct or common sense leaves it?" No, he says, and "when anybody undertakes to

37

say *precisely* what that order consists in, he will quickly find he outruns all logical warrant" (376). A more contemporary and perhaps tangential example of this proposition can be found in the voice of Bruce Springsteen. In an interview about his song "Tenth Avenue Freeze-Out," he says, laughing, "I still don't know to this day what that really means.... But it's important." Smiling and wagging a finger, he says again, "It's important" (Springsteen). He's never been able to precisely define that phrase, "Tenth Avenue Freeze-Out," but he knows it gets at the heart of something significant. When it comes to the writing process (whether it's Springsteen or the rest of us), we often live and work, especially at the beginning, in just this kind of uncertainty. Or, as Ann Berthoff says, "The first use of language that a student of composition has to learn, I think, is in the generation of chaos. If we don't begin there, we falsify the composition process because composition requires choosing all along the way, and you can't choose if there are no perceived alternatives: chaos is the source of alternatives" (75). "Chaos is [also] scary," Berthoff admits, but what "we must realize ourselves and make dramatically evident to our students is what I. A. Richards means when he calls ambiguities 'the hinges of thought'" (71). Thus, though they may move in different spheres, Peirce, Springsteen, and Berthoff can help student writers move away from the certainty of theists and atheists in the composition classroom and towards a search, at least in the beginning, to discover what religion does for us in the world; as teachers we can then help students focus their argumentative energies *there* instead of on preconceived, well-ingrained, infallible notions of what religion is.

Peirce's preference that God remain rather vaguely described instead of precisely defined comes with a sense of hybridity that he says must be understood and acknowledged as well. That is, to use terms more familiar in a contemporary composition course, we need not view believers and non-believers as polar opposites or political enemies who share nothing in common. "The love that God is," Peirce argues, "is not a love of which hatred is the contrary; otherwise Satan would be a coordinate power; but it is a love which embraces hatred as an imperfect stage of it" (*Philosophy* 362). Such a hybrid approach to one's understanding of the world—that, for instance, secular and religious perspectives are part and parcel of each other—can help provide a fresh and useful understanding of the "other side" by suggesting that we view science as an imperfect stage of faith and faith as an imperfect stage of science. And for Peirce, it all involves social responsibility, for "self-love is no love" (362). Separated camps usually lead to what we have already seen as the "Gospel of Greed." He reminds us that "the movement of love is circular [with] the same impulse projecting creations into independency and drawing them into harmony." And we can't forget that "love is not directed to abstractions but to persons," to our neighbors, to those we share this planet with right now (362).

Peirce offers as well what he calls a Neglected Argument concerning the question of God, an argument closely connected to that of avoiding precision and embracing the vague. He promotes the notion of Pure Play, which "involves no purpose save that of casting aside all serious purpose" and which "has no rules, except this very law of liberty. It bloweth where it listeth" (*Charles* 360). Tapping into the value of what might be called the pleasure of letting go, he writes, "One who sits down with the purpose of becoming convinced of the truth of religion ... can never attain the entirety even of a physicist's belief in electrons" (360). As Emerson says that "books are for the scholar's idle time" and as many composition teachers urge their students to freewrite and brainstorm, Peirce tells us to set aside the direction we receive from priests, parents, or books, and instead "enter your skiff of Musement, push off into the lake of thought, and leave the breath of heaven to swell your sail. With your eyes open, awake to what is about or within you, and open conversation with yourself" (362).

When it comes to both science and religion, we inevitably run into propositions that don't seem very likely. Casting off as Peirce suggests helps to keep the mind open, "to dismiss doubts on the matter from consideration" (*Charles* 400). Dismissing doubts from the process of inquiry here means *giving the proposition at hand every opportunity.* "There is a vast difference," Peirce notes, "between that and any holding of the proposition for certain. To hold a proposition for certain is to puff oneself up with the vanity of perfect knowledge. It leaves no room for Faith" (400). To pursue in the sense he suggests means to inquire by allowing for the possibility of a proposition without any reservation, a perspective that allows for greater possibilities, not fewer. Anticipating criticism, Peirce offers the following example: "But you may ask, don't you admit there are any delusions? Yes: I may think a thing is black, and on close examination it may turn out to be bottle-green. But I cannot think a thing is black if there is no such thing to be seen as black" (*Philosophy* 378).

Peirce's Neglected Argument and focus on exploration and possibility fit with his overall pragmatic perspective based on experience, contingency, and reflection upon the consequences of our beliefs—a perspective that allows student writers to imagine a fresh number of possibilities when it comes to negotiating reason and religion. Or, as Peirce puts such a comingling another way, "logic depends on a mere struggle to escape doubt, which, as it terminates in action, must begin in emotion" (*Collected Papers* 2:655). As we write and wrestle with these enormous subjects, we do well to keep in mind the underlying maxim of Peirce's pragmatism: to consider "what effects, that might conceivably have practical bearings, we conceive the object of our conception to have" (5: 401–2). In other words, to prompt our students to consider that, for instance, religion is what it does in the world.

William James: Running the Gauntlet

Of the three key pragmatists I discuss in this book, William James has the most to say about religion. In addition to his substantial *Varieties of Religious Experience* and influential essays such as "Will to Believe," the topic of religion appears throughout the corpus of his work. In *Pragmatism*, for example, where he outlines and develops the method Peirce established, God and religion get a lot of attention. He notes, in fact, that "the principle of Peirce, the principle of pragmatism ... lay entirely unnoticed by anyone for twenty years, until I ... brought it forward again and made a special application of it to religion" (24).

James was constantly grappling with the way in which religious belief occupied our lives. As Bennett Ramsey notes,

> I see James as absorbed, throughout most of his work, with the investigation and consideration of religious problems. More to the point, I see him attempting to broaden the definition of religion beyond the confines of theistic and supernaturalistic frameworks toward immanentist, almost naturalistic meaning. Above all, I see James as advocating a religious way of life, a way of being based not on control, but on

40

respect for and responsibility to the immanent ties and powers that bind the self [3].

It is this sort of pragmatic approach to concepts of God and religion that can be highly effective in the composition course: an approach that is based not on the controlling definitions of what God and religion *are* but on an awareness of the changing forces within oneself and in relation to others. Like his predecessor Peirce, James applies this approach through the tools of his own expertise. While Peirce worked from his roots in science and mathematics, James developed his pragmatism through the fields of psychology and education to explore what religious belief does for us as opposed to being hobbled by what Ramsey calls "the confines of theistic and supernaturalistic frameworks."

With respect to teaching, James' *Talks to Teachers on Psychology; and to Students on Some of Life's Ideals* is a place to start for composition teachers in the twenty-first century. In this book, James tries to free the profession of education from some of the stringent and confining regulation that bedevils it still. To begin, he says, "Teaching is an art" (23), so there can be no one formula for its successful practice. In addition, he offers the then radical notion of approaching our students as *whole* people. "My main desire," he states, "has been to make [teachers] conceive, and, if possible, reproduce sympathetically in their imagination, the mental life of their pupil as the sort of active unity which he himself feels it to be. *He* doesn't chop himself up into distinct processes and compartments" (18). James describes the human being as essentially an organism constantly reacting to a barrage of impressions, and education, he suggests, "*is little more than a mass of possibilities of reaction*, acquired at home, at school, or in the training of affairs. The teacher's task is that of supervising the acquiring process" (42).

Especially pertinent to our discussion of religion in the writing class is, I believe, his notion that "*every acquired reaction is, as a rule, either a complication grafted on a native reaction, or a substitute for a native reaction*" (42). James develops this notion nicely in *Pragmatism* with a cooking metaphor, arguing that all of our new truths must be gradually "stewed down with the sauce of the old" (75). What is paramount, however, on the teacher's part is that in attempting to graft new knowledge onto the old, or stew fresh complications down into well-worn native reactions, the teacher must attempt to have a grasp of those native reactions that have long been in place. "The teacher's art," James posits, "consists in bringing about the substitution or complication, and success in the art presupposes a sympathetic acquaintance with the reactive tendencies natively there" (42). While it's neither possible nor desirable to be acquainted with all the native reactive tendencies of all of our students, many secular academics—myself included—may do well to foster a more "sympathetic acquaintance" with the mass of "reactive tendencies" we know to be already there in our students when unearthing religion.

To do so, James suggests that teachers first consider for a moment the reverence we have for reason and logic. Like Peirce, he places a premium on the connection between what we feel and what we reason: "Our judgments concerning the worth of things, big or little, depend on the *feelings* the things arouse in us. Where we judge a thing to be precious in consequence of the *idea* we frame of it, this is only because the idea is itself associated already with a feeling" (149). In the concluding chapter of *Talks to Teachers*, James draws upon Tolstoy to emphasize the point: "The more we live by our intellect, the less we understand the meaning of life" (179). To put it another way, as we tend to tell our composition students when talking about the rhetorical triangle, logos is only one part of the puzzle.

If it is true that the *idea* of a thing and its associated feelings must be dealt with together, then the idea of religion and the associated feelings gathered from a student's past experiences with religion must also be taken together. But how does one prevent these associated feelings or "native reactive tendencies" from clouding and overwhelming a student's essay? When we work with rigid definitions of religion, we invite dogmatism and intolerance of conflicting beliefs. James suggests that instead of discussing religious belief, *per se*, the actual choice to believe, or, equally important, not to believe, may be a more fruitful focus.

According to James, choosing between believing and not believing—and it is an active choice—is a *forced option*. He defines "option" as the decision one makes between two hypotheses, and an option becomes real if it is "forced," where we absolutely have to choose. He explains, "If I say to you: 'Choose between going out with your umbrella or without it,' I do not offer you a genuine option, for it is not forced.

You can easily avoid it by not going out at all.... But if I say, 'Either accept this truth or go without it,' I put on you a forced option, for there is no standing place outside the alternative" (89). Choosing not to believe, James argues, is as active a choice as choosing to believe. The nonbeliever "is actively playing his stake as much as the believer is; he is backing the field against the religious hypothesis, just as the believer is backing the religious hypothesis against the field" (106). Finally, and perhaps the most important for those in a composition course, is the distinction he makes between a living option and a dead option.

> A living option is one where both hypotheses are live ones. If I say to you: "Be a theosophist or be a Mohammedan," it is probably a dead option, because for you neither hypothesis is likely to be alive. But if I say, "Be an agnostic or be a Christian," it is otherwise: trained as you are, each hypothesis makes some appeal, however small, to your belief [89].

The trouble, though, practically speaking, is getting theists and atheists to acknowledge the hypothesis they didn't choose as a *live* one—producing living options on the question of God—so that real dialogue and understanding is feasible. And whether or not a hypothesis is seen as live or dead depends not on some inherent trait in the hypothesis itself, but rather on the actual experiences of the individual. The "deadness and liveness in an hypothesis are not intrinsic properties, but relations to the individual thinker" (89).

Considering the choice that we are all faced with when it comes to religion, James pays homage to the element of possibility and uncertainty. He rejects the dogmatic absolutist as well as the adamant atheist: "I cannot willfully agree to keep my willing nature out of the game. I cannot do so for this plain reason, that *a rule of thinking which would absolutely prevent me from acknowledging certain kinds of truth if those kinds of truth were really there, would be an irrational rule*" ("Will" 107). Religious belief, in other words, should be understood as a living, possible hypothesis, worthy of consideration yet subject to the same pragmatic critique as any of our other contending beliefs. So while "the idea of Him seems even to exert a positively paralyzing effect on the mind" of a non-believer, this effect does not render the hypothesis dead. And, for the believer, it is necessary to understand that claims to divine experiences are "like all other human experiences" in that "they too certainly share in the general liability to illusion and mistake" (*Pragmatism* 85). The words "maybe" and "some" need to be entertained more by everyone, he suggests, as all too often "the only categories universally consistent and therefore pertinent to reality are 'all' and 'none'" (*Pragmatism* 122). For as our daily experiences have consistently shown, "the next turn in events can at any given moment genuinely be ambiguous, i.e., possibly this, but also possibly that" (130).

I see James' position on both the possibilities and limits of religion as critically important to teaching our students how to moderate their natural tendencies to absolutism and dogmatism as they frame their essays and discuss their ideas with each other. What better insight into belief, its natural limits as well as its possible heights, can guide us? It demonstrates that our beliefs in anything—whether it be a religion, a person, a political ideal, or even a dietary supplement or engine additive—must be seen for what they are, products of the human mind. One might argue that belief in God or the "true faith" of one's choosing is the exception because its source is divine and not human, but James and other American Pragmatists can teach us that that is not true. Even if we allow for the possibility that the god in which one believes or the faith to which he or she adheres might have divine origin, the choice to believe in that god or that faith is necessarily a human construct. It belongs to the individual man or woman who holds, nourishes, and tests it. It is therefore subject, as James says, to the same limitations of any other human experience—"the general liability to illusion and mistake."

If we wish to convince our students, then, to be respectful of the belief systems that their neighbors and peers have chosen, we must show them, first, that the very act of believing in such systems is their own human choice and, second, that human choices are subject to the kinds of imperfections identified by William James and other pragmatists. Recognizing such limitations is not only realistic and pragmatic, but it is also intellectually liberating for ourselves and our students. We are no longer faced with the obligation to find—no matter what the obstacles—a justification for absolute and predetermined articles of faith. We, and our students, are now free to explore both the limitations and possibilities of faith based on the impact that it has on the ethical behavior or misbehavior of human beings. This, of course, begins to answer the question, "What can religion do?"

Imbedded in James' emphasis on possibility is always the idea that we might actually be right about something, but that is different from *knowing* that we are right. "To *know* is one thing, and to know for certain *that* we know is another" (James, "Will" 96). This doctrine cautions both sides. It warns the dogmatic absolutist that while he *may* be right, there is yet no evidence (or at least not enough) to confirm the fact. It also warns the atheistic absolutist that while she too *may* be right, the argument that there is yet no evidence to confirm the existence of God does not altogether bar His or Her being. It is important to keep these parameters in mind as we tell our students that a debate over the existence of God cannot be pursued in a composition course because the Jamesean element of continuing possibility will inevitably reduce such a debate to the inconclusive.

This notion of continuing possibility is illustrated in James' discussion of the ultimate salvation of the world, a tenet embraced by several religions. "What does it pragmatically mean to say that this is possible?" he asks. "It means that some of the conditions of the world's deliverance do actually exist. The more of them there are existent, the fewer preventing conditions you can find, the better-grounded is the salvation's possibility, the more *probable* does the fact of the deliverance become" (125). But, importantly, this deliverance can only remain within the *realm of possibility*, going no further, at best, than *the probable*. The opposite possibility is also continually true: i.e., that of the destruction of the world. As numerous doomsayers have proved to their own undoubted dismay, the dates they have predicted for the end of the world continue to come and go with the world paying little attention. Of course, this is not to say that it will never end, only that we are unable to know this with certainty. As Hamlet famously advises, "we defy augury: there's a special providence in the fall of a sparrow. If it be now, 'tis not to come; if it not to come, it will be now ... the readiness is all" (5.2 219–222).

Indeed, we cannot know with certainty; we only know of the possibility. And that possibility is actually multiplied within the endless limits of human imagination. So what do we do with all of these pragmatic possibilities? We pit them against each other. "In other words," James writes, "the greatest enemy of any one of our truths may be the rest of our truths" (*Pragmatism* 37). Again, a staple of this approach is that all of our beliefs must run the gauntlet of all our other beliefs (37).

With respect to the notion of God's existence, James was inclined to accept it, but not deferentially: "now whatever its residual difficulties may be, experience shows that [the hypothesis of God] certainly does work, and that the problem is to build it out and determine it so that it will combine satisfactorily with all the other working truths" (131). To try to reach a satisfactory combination and to promote productive writing and dialogue in the composition course, we can turn back to the idea of usefulness.

To see if something is useful, we can look to a central pragmatic question as James frames it: What practical difference would it make to someone if this notion rather than that notion were true? The roots of the notion are irrelevant; this question is only concerned with the end result. It is not, as James puts it, "where it comes from, but what it leads to." For a pragmatist, as I mentioned in chapter 1, it makes no difference "from what quarter a hypothesis may come to him: he may have acquired it by fair means or by foul; passion may have whispered or accident suggested it" (99). And as our possible truths spar with one another for supremacy, "which may be treated as the *more* true depends altogether on the human use of it" (111). For "they have, indeed, no meaning and no reality if they have no use" (118).

And the human use of it is understood in social, communal terms. At the outset of *Principles of Psychology*, James' early and perhaps most influential work, he casts his portrait of the self in individual terms. By the end of the book, however, and for the remainder of his career, the individual self is understood—must be understood—in a social context. As Bennett Ramsey notes, in the final section of *Principles* James "added a background image to the primary processes; he replaced the self not just back into its nascent state but into a social world. Or rather, he replaced the self back into a socially unstable world, a world without boundaries" (48). James was well aware that to conceive of the self in isolation "was an abstraction." From this point in his career the self would be set "in the world where James' readers lived, where all sorts of selves were at work" (48), a setting that's in line with the collaborative and real-world approach that many twenty-first-century composition teachers take in the classroom.

By the time James delivered his lectures which comprise *The Varieties of Religious Experience*, religious experience was not at all conceived, developed, and named from *within* an individual, but rather from *without*. Much as Lev Vygotsky argued a few years later, James proposed that we do not first look inward for meaning and then project out to the world; we look outward first, and develop our individual meanings and knowledge from our surroundings. And our conceptions of religious belief are no different: "religious love is only man's natural emotion of love directed to a religious object; religious fear is only the ordinary fear of commerce, so to speak, the common quaking of the human breast" expressed in relation to one's environment (*Varieties* 36). As Vygotsky suggests in *Thought and Language*, "The word is a thing in our consciousness ... that is absolutely impossible for one person, but that becomes a reality for two" (256). So, too, does James suggest that a personal, individual relationship with God, *once articulated*, becomes crudely defined by dominant, pre-existing, public descriptions that can only have meaning in relation to others. And as religion for James was no longer "a path of detachment and privacy but a route of radical and public commitment" (Ramsey 137), our religious responsibility became a responsibility to other people rather than to an ultimate, private, abstract Truth.

Importantly, James is critical of the believer who merely "follows the conventional observances of his country, whether it be Buddhist, Christian, or Mohammedan" (*Varieties* 19). True religion, he says, results from those who come to it via individual experiences "not as a dull habit but as an acute fever" (19). If composition teachers wish to encourage their students to write about religious experience or the work that religion can accomplish in their lives and the lives of others, they, too, should remember that experience and imitation are very different things. We should encourage our students to beware of parroting received articles or dogma. Speak from experience. For James, there is also a distinct difference between the sick soul and the religiously healthy-minded individual. The name of the latter is purposely misleading to imply a naïve, oblivious optimism which is based on avoidance and which doesn't offer us much we can use. It is the sick-souled individual, for whom religion is an "acute fever" rather than a "dull habit," whose religious experiences are worth examining because they include *the whole* of experience. The sick-soul is more acutely aware of the circumstances that surround us. A touch of the morbid, in fact, is a necessary element rather than something to be shunned. The healthy-minded, James argues, effectively ignore those experiences they find distasteful—a practice that has been encouraged by one dominant religion in much of the Western world. "The Catholic practice of confession and absolution is little more than a systematic method of keeping healthy-mindedness on top" and of continuously allowing one to start a "clean page with no old debts inscribed. Any Catholic will tell us how clean and fresh and free he feels after the purging operation" (*Varieties* 120).

For James, such an approach is akin to Pollyanna in denial, so he determines to "resolutely turn our backs on ... their sky-blue optimistic gospel." With tough but realistic purpose, he prefers to see "whether pity, pain, and fear, and the sentiment of human helplessness may not open a profounder view" (126). Hardly popular in an old-fashioned "revival" or in the celebratory songs of praise that some of our students will have grown from, this Jamesean seriousness may nonetheless serve us well in that it can open awareness to a "profounder view" of the sometimes despairing human condition.

So where do we find those sick souls from whose searing experiences we might learn? James says we need look no further than to our own everyday lives and those of the people around us. Like Emerson, who tells us that if books are used in place of experience they become "noxious" and the guide "a tyrant," James insists that any absolute, unwavering doctrine is "but the old story, of a useful practice first becoming a method, then a habit, and finally a tyranny that defeats the end it was used for" (*Pluralistic* 99). Also like Emerson, who advises us to explore "the familiar, the common and the low," James tells us at the very outset of *Varieties* that what "we shall find most instructive need not then be sought for in the haunts of special erudition—they lie along the beaten highway" (3). "Pragmatism," he writes, "is willing to take anything, to follow either logic or the senses and to count the humblest and most personal experiences. She will count mystical experiences if they have practical consequences. She will take a God who lives in the very dirt of private fact—if that should seem a likely place to find Him" (*Pragmatism* 38).

Not surprisingly, James drew a fair amount of criticism for practicing what he preached. In *Principles*, as in most of his other work, he relied a great deal on simple, unsubstantiated testimony from lay people, drawing his conclusions more often than not from their observations as "nonprofessionals." Many, including Charles Peirce, felt that conclusions based on such "data" were suspect at best. Others, however, appreciated his departure from the generally accepted scientific method. John Dewey comments, for example, that James' approach offers invaluable insight as it allows him to explore "genuine events, events that most persons are too conventional or too literal to notice at all" (Flower 642).

For James, underlying the importance of all these everyday experiences is the mandate that it is impossible to hold anything for certain beforehand: you have to wade through the world. "You cannot enter the phenomenal world with the notion of it in your grasp, and name beforehand any detail which you are likely to meet there" (*Pluralistic* 61). This, in turn, brings us back to the notion of possibility and contingency. Like Peirce, James saw everything as "a product of contingency and time" (Ramsey 12). We find ourselves, then, with a pluralistic view of the world, a view which allows "that there *may* be one sovereign purpose, system, kind, and story," but that "it is rash to affirm this dogmatically without better evidence than we possess at present" (*Pragmatism* 65). Hence, the pragmatic method,

> pending the final empirical ascertainment of just what the balance of union and disunion among things may be, must obviously arrange herself along the pluralistic side. Some day, she admits, even total union, with one knower, one origin, and a universe consolidated in every conceivable way, may turn out to be the most acceptable of all hypotheses. Meanwhile the opposite hypothesis, of a world imperfectly unified still, and perhaps always to remain so, must be sincerely entertained [72].

Part of this pluralistic view is the notion that pragmatism serves as "a happy harmonizer of empiricist ways of thinking with the more religious demands of human beings" (33). James compares two opposite types of what he calls "mental make-ups," the Tender-Minded (those who are idealistic, optimistic, religious, free-willist, monistic, dogmatical) and the Tough-Minded (materialistic, pessimistic, irreligious, fatalistic, pluralistic, skeptical). His labels may seem curious, but his purpose is to find a bridge between two vastly different and influential perspectives on our place in the world. He sees that the sides "have a low opinion of each other" and that "each type believes the other to be inferior" (*Pragmatism* 9).

The mediating bridge that he searches for is that of pragmatism, whose primary function "'unstiffens' our theories. She has in fact no prejudices whatsoever, no obstructive dogmas, no rigid canons.... She is completely genial. She will entertain any hypothesis" (*Pragmatism* 38). Above all, for James pragmatism "is a method only" which "does not stand for any special results" (25).

This may at first be hard to accept, as most of us are accustomed to wanting a particular outcome. By implication, then, the method asks us to give up a certain amount of control, and to really give ourselves over to the idea that an experience tomorrow or in twenty years *might* change our entire world-view. It's important to remember that being wrong is not only acceptable, but often useful. "Our errors are surely not such awfully solemn things," James suggests. "In a world where we are so certain to incur them, in spite of all our caution, a certain lightness of heart seems healthier than ... excessive nervousness on their behalf" ("Will" 100). Or, as Michael Jordan has said, "I have failed over and over and over again, and that is why I succeed" (Murray 1).

Such is the process of learning—a process that is more often than not "strained, and sometimes painfully so, between ... older beliefs and the novelties which experience brings along" ("Will" 74). And to go back to James' cooking metaphor I mentioned at the start of this section, it's also a process in which growth happens

> in spots; and like grease-spots, the spots spread. But we let them spread as little as possible, we keep unaltered as much of our old knowledge, as many of our old prejudices and beliefs as we can. We patch and tinker more than we renew ... it happens relatively seldom that the new fat is added *raw*. More usually it is embedded cooked, as one might say. Or stewed down in the sauce of the old [74–75].

Religion serves as a base for the lives of many students, a base of knowledge from which they respond to the world and to which new notions must be added and stirred with some care. It also serves as a convenient target for those who don't believe. In addressing religion as a social and political issue in the writing class, we can't give it a free pass, but we can give it the same chance as anything else to make its claim as a useful means for improving our lives. And we can do that by avoiding any metaphysical discussions and looking instead to the palpable effects, based on human experience, that religious belief has here on earth.

John Dewey: Reframing the Question

John Dewey's pragmatism, like the pragmatism of Peirce and James, owes a great deal to Emerson. Dewey was inspired by the way in which Emerson "takes the distinctions and classifications which to most philosophers are true in and of and because of their systems, and makes them true of life, of the common experience" of everyday people (Dewey, "Ralph Waldo Emerson" 73–74). He pointed out Emerson's constant "reference to immediate life" and the way in which Emerson held the thinking of all the great philosophers accountable to "present and immediate experience" (74). Building upon James and Peirce, Dewey developed Emerson's initial notions of experience, action, and social responsibility to eventually become not only one of America's greatest philosophers but also the colossal figure who transformed our approach to education. His work spans nearly a century, and taken as a whole, pedagogy emerges as a central concern; specifically, the way in which pedagogy can help effect democratic change on the streets of the United States. With respect to pragmatism, Cornel West argues that after Dewey, "to be a pragmatist is to be a social critic, literary critic, or a poet—in short, a participant in cultural criticism and cultural creation" (*American Evasion* 71). West adds that "John Dewey is the culmination of the tradition of American pragmatism" and that he "helps us see the complex and mediated ways in which philosophical problems are linked to societal crises" (71).

Social context was critical to Dewey's philosophy, especially to his philosophy of education. He witnessed unprecedented change in his country—a rapid transformation from a primarily agricultural Republic to one of the first industrialized, manufacturing nations in the world. This revolution brought with it as well an overwhelming population boom that served in large part to support this new way of life. The circumstances surrounding this new way of life, though, were often atrocious; working and living conditions led, for most, to poverty, injury, and disease. In Dewey's mind, the role of education should be first and foremost directed at improving these conditions. He felt that the school was primarily "a social institution," and that "education being a social process, the school is simply a form of community life in which all those agencies are concentrated that will be most effective in bringing [the student] to share in the inherited resources of the race, and to use his own powers for social ends" (*Philosophy* 445). In this regard, school should always be continuous with the rest of life.

Dewey was wary that as "formal teaching and training grow in extent, there is the danger of creating an undesirable split between the experience gained in more direct associations and what is acquired in school" (*Democracy* 9). As Emerson reminds us that books are for "the scholar's idle time," so too does Dewey remind us that "the true center of correlation on the school subjects is not science, nor literature, nor history, nor geography, but the child's own social activities" (*Philosophy* 448). In other words, what we do in the classroom should have everything to do with what our students actually do in the world, such as going to church and praying to God.

Like Peirce and James, Dewey saw lived experience as playing an integral part in the learning process. "All genuine education comes about through experience" (507), he writes. And similar to Paulo Freire's critique of the "banking method" of education where knowledge is simply deposited into the passive minds of students and then regurgitated without engagement or retention, Dewey outlines "two senses of the word 'learning'":

> On the one hand, learning is the sum total of what is known, as that is handed down by books and learned men. It is something external, an accumulation of cognitions as one might store material commodities in a warehouse. Truth exists ready-made somewhere. Study is then the process by which an individual draws on what is in storage. On the other hand, learning means something which the individual *does* when he studies. It is an active, personally conducted affair [*Democracy* 334–335].

For Dewey, this second approach, the "active, personally conducted affair," has the best chance of instilling in students the desire to continue learning on their own after they've left the classroom.

With respect to forming and adjusting our beliefs, Dewey draws on Peirce in arguing that "it is the characteristic use to which the thing is put, because of its specific qualities, which supplies the meaning with which it is identified" (*Democracy* 29). Again, to know what something is, look to what it does in the world. The next step is to ask how it is useful, or not useful, for improving the human condition. And as James writes that pragmatism will take any route to knowledge as long as the outcome proves useful, Dewey too insists that all types of experience and all kinds of means are necessary in the pursuit of useful truths. "There is something both ridiculous and disconcerting," he writes, about the way in which we have convinced ourselves "to infer that scientific ways of thinking of objects give the inner reality of things, and that they put a mark of spuriousness upon all other ways of thinking them, and of perceiving and enjoying them" (*Quest for Certainty* 135–36). Dewey is critical of institutions like organized religion, but he is adamant that we can not summarily exclude a possible way of knowing, and, conversely, that "there is no kind of inquiry which has a monopoly of the honorable title of knowledge" (220). As Peirce said in a reference to Jesus, Dewey says too that no matter how we arrive at our truths, it is "by their fruits we shall know them" (220).

Like Susanne Langer, Dewey tried to ground our approach to science, philosophy, religion, and education by suggesting we take a step back to reevaluate the questions we're asking. Regarding philosophy, he argues that we need to get to a point where it "ceases to be a device for dealing with the problems of philosophers and becomes a method, cultivated by philosophers, for dealing with the problems of men" ("Need" 66–67). This vein of criticism is perhaps most persuasively put in his influential essay "The Need for a Recovery of Philosophy," first published in 1917. Dewey's principle complaint is that philosophy is mired in questions that are no longer pertinent; he begins by stating that the essay may

> be looked upon as an attempt to forward the emancipation of philosophy from too intimate and exclusive attachment to traditional problems. It is not in intent a criticism of various solutions that have been offered, but raises a question *as to the genuineness, under the present conditions of science and social life, of the problems* [21].

Again like Langer, Dewey asks, "Is it not time that philosophers turned from the attempt to determine the comparative merits of various replies to the questions to a consideration of the claims of the questions?" (43). And to question our questions in this sense, we return, as always, to experience. In this same essay, Dewey offers the following definition of experience:

> Experience is primarily a process of undergoing: a process of standing something; of suffering and passion, of affection, in the literal sense of

53

these words. The organism has to endure, to undergo, the consequence of its own actions. Experience, in other words, is a matter of
simultaneous doings and sufferings.... And experience is not identical
with brain action; it is the entire organic agent-patient in all its interaction with the environment, natural and social [25–26].

In addition, Dewey explores how we gain knowledge from experience
by citing experience as "ways of doing and suffering" and knowledge as
"discovering what particular mode—qualitatively unique—of doing and
suffering it is" (45). To gain knowledge, then, we must actively work to
understand our experience. He also asserts that modern philosophy
tends to offer ideas "*forced into* experience, not *gathered from* it" (45).

Much of what Dewey says in "The Need for a Recovery of Philosophy" about the nature of experience and the need to question our questions serves as a base for his discussion on religion in *A Common Faith*,
published almost two decades later. This little book (scarcely a book, at
less than 90 pages) is one that every composition teacher should read.
In it, Dewey does not disavow religious belief; on the contrary, he tries
to make it stronger. But he is often misunderstood as trivializing religion
because his central claim in *A Common Faith* is that religion's continued
association with the supernatural has, in the modern day, drained it of
its power and its usefulness. We need, he says, to stop concerning ourselves with how to keep responding to the supernatural premise of religious belief and instead turn our focus to the premise itself. He suggests
that "the religious element in life has been hampered by conceptions of
the supernatural that were imbedded in those cultures wherein man had
little control over outer nature and little in the way of sure inquiry and
test." Science and time have greatly changed our understanding of the
world, but Dewey emphasizes that "this change is not fatal to the religious values in our common experience, however adverse its impact
may be upon historic religions" (*Common* 56). The religious attitude,
he suggests, has the possibility of doing so much for us, but it must be
freed from its metaphysical baggage.

Before exploring his argument concerning the supernatural, however, we should back up to the beginning of his book for some context
and definitions. Many of us might find the very first sentence, in fact,
to sound sadly familiar: "Never before in history has mankind been so
much of two minds, so divided into two camps, as it is today" (1). The

entire first page, actually, speaks in terms of division and opposition. He describes one camp as filled with those who believe that religious belief in any form must necessarily be associated with the supernatural, and he describes the other camp as including those who believe that since science has discredited the supernatural claims of religion, it has nothing at all to offer. Dewey attempts to forge a middle ground by relieving religious belief of the supernatural, a middle ground he acknowledges will irritate both sides. It will be attacked, he says, by the first group as undercutting "the vital nerve of the religious element itself" and by the second group as "a timid half-way position," an irresponsible "concession and compromise ... an emotional hangover from childhood indoctrination" (3). The rest of the book works to assuage these misgivings, beginning with his initial definition of religion, and his distinction between "religion" and "religious."

Much as Peirce and James describe religious belief, Dewey says, "We are forced to acknowledge that concretely there is no such thing as religion in the singular. There is only a multitude of religions. 'Religion' is a strictly collective term" (7). Any attempts to pin it down will inevitably prove to be "too much or too little" (7). Having said that, Dewey draws a sharp distinction between "religion" as a noun and "religious" as an adjective. The former, he says,

> always signifies a special body of beliefs and practices having some kind of institutional organization, loose or tight. In contrast, the adjective "religious" denotes nothing in the way of a specifiable entity, either institutional or as a system of beliefs. It does not denote anything to which one can specifically point as one can point to this and that historic religion or existing church. For it does not denote anything that can exist by itself or that can be organized into a particular and distinctive form of existence [10].

Existing "by itself" is a critical difference. A religious attitude, unencumbered by worship of the supernatural, can operate freely in conjunction with the rest of life. The drawback of religion as an institution, Dewey argues, is that it often separates itself from the rest of life, and it does so in large part by relying on the supernatural. He says, for instance,

> It is of the nature of a religion based on the supernatural to draw a line between the religious and the secular and the profane, even when it asserts the rightful authority of the Church and its religion to dominate

these other interests. The conception that "religious" signifies a certain attitude and outlook, independent of the supernatural, necessitates no such division. It does not shut religious values up within a particular compartment [66].

An example of this point can be seen in one church's contemporary struggle over what to do with homosexuality. The Episcopal church recently appointed for the first time a female presiding bishop, Katherine Jefferts Schori. Bishop Schori's acceptance of homosexuality and same-sex marriage represents a growing number of worshipers who are inclined to exhibit a *religious* attitude when it comes to the topic of same-sex relationships, loosening it from the grip of *religion* which often relies on the official word of God to draw its rather rigid conclusions. More and more, as supporters of same-sex marriage gain ground, we hear a religious attitude, based on lived experience, from believers and non-believers alike—the nickel tends to drop when they realize they actually know gays and lesbians who they love and respect. Keeping Dewey's grammar-based distinction in mind, we can encourage composition students to focus, for instance, on the way in which a particular church reacts to or helps to shape cultural norms and practices in a particular community.

Dewey notes that a primary problem with religion's connection to the supernatural is that while it works to validate an other-worldly condition, definite claims are made apart from actual experience (and then, in many cases, those claims are forced into experience). As a result, what occurs is a subtle and dubious shift from religious faith to intellectual certainty. "It is argued," Dewey writes,

> That the ideal is already the final reality at the heart of things that exist, and that only our senses or the corruption of our natures prevent us from apprehending its prior existential being. Starting, say, from such an idea as that justice is more than a moral ideal because it is embedded in the very make-up of the actually existent world, men have gone on to build up vast intellectual schemes, philosophies, and theologies, to prove that ideals are real not as ideals but as antecedently existing actualities [21].

In building up such philosophies and theologies, Dewey argues that these claims no longer inhabit the world of faith, but rather inhabit—or try to inhabit—the world of intellectual reason. For as he notes, "Faith that something should be in existence as far as lies in our power *is changed* into the intellectual belief that it is already in existence" (21–22). The result is that an individual's active pursuit for an ideal is blunted as it has already been provided as a static intellectual fact. And when actual experiences differ from these pre-existing facts, reliance on the supernatural slips seamlessly into play—it's not for us to know, it's beyond our grasp, etc. When it comes to the essence of God, any kind of intellectual certainty is best left at the door by believers and nonbelievers alike when entering the contemporary composition course.

According to Dewey, when religion puts supernatural proposals in intellectual terms, religion itself becomes a substitute for knowledge, enabling it to work against rather than with the rest of our lives. Quoting John Locke, Dewey notes that in this regard, "faith is 'assent to a proposition … on the credit of its proposer.' Religious faith is then given to a body of propositions as true on the credit of their supernatural author, reason coming in to demonstrate the reasonableness of giving such credit" (20). Religion can often find itself, then, using reason to convince us that we shouldn't demand a better reason, resting its supernatural claims on intellectual acquiescence rather than faith. To avoid this kind of direction altogether in the composition class, we can let students know that they are welcome to explore the many reasons for being religious or nonreligious that their own life experiences have taught them. However, they should be careful not to use such reasons to make fixed supernatural claims—in the guise of intellectual facts—that none of us can presently prove.

In the work of C. S. Lewis, one of the most prominent Christian apologists of the modern era, we can see an example of the shift from faith to intellectual certainty that Dewey describes. Based on the evidence he found in this world, Lewis drew the logical conclusion that God exists and that the Christian proposition is true. Once we understand God's plan, Lewis proposed, a reasonable case can be made in favor of Him. For instance, in response to the common argument by skeptics that a loving, omniscient, omnipotent God would not allow suffering in the world, Lewis says we need to properly understand the role that suffering plays: God allows us to suffer so we may become better creatures, morally enlightened and, ultimately, happy (*Problem* 110). What, then, a skeptic might ask, about the suffering of infants and young children, who don't have the capacity for understanding or for learning from what happens to them? The adults around those children will benefit, Lewis and others respond, and, while they don't know it at the time, the children themselves may draw on that experience later in life (see Wielenberg 50–51). But what if...? And so on, and so on. Such discussions may have, and have had, no end. What is clear, however, is that we are no longer in the realm of faith. This exchange is based on logic and reason. We have moved, as Dewey put it, from faith that something should exist (goodness/kindness/loving intention) to the intellectual claim that it already exists in perfect form.

One problem with this move can be seen by taking the same example of suffering. If God lets us suffer for our own spiritual and moral development, then, logically, humans may think it's ok for them to inflict suffering on others for that very same purpose. Defenders of Lewis argue that the infliction of suffering for moral development is within the purview of God alone—humans are unable to see when and why such action should be taken (Petrik 51–52). That makes sense. But along these lines, experience has shown us that many human beings are likely to make the if-then inference stated above (if God does it, so can we) without considering the distinction offered by Lewis' defenders. On the other hand, people are, of course, convinced to do good in the world based on logical arguments of divine intention. In either case, this is not where we want to be as we're now in the world of intellectual and ontological truth regarding the supernatural rather than the world of contingency based on lived experience. The latter is far more manageable in a secular composition course. For instance, the topic of capital punishment in the first-year writing course elicits religious arguments for such a law ("an eye for an eye") and against such a law ("vengeance is mine, sayeth the Lord"). The comp class is not the place for resolving intellectual arguments regarding the right interpretation of God's intent with respect to state-sanctioned murder. Our focus should be on the practical consequences of having this law on our books.

Another example of an intellectual argument concerning the truth about God is C. S. Lewis' famous "Trilemma," which is often read as making the following claim. Given what we know about Jesus and his preaching, he would have to have been either crazy or the Devil himself. Lewis concluded that it was obvious "He was neither a lunatic or a fiend;

and *consequently*, however strange or terrifying or unlikely it may seem, I have to accept the view that He was and is God" (*Mere Christianity*, 52–53, italics mine). In the first-year composition course, many of us talk about various kinds of reasoning: deductive, inductive, etc. Many things can go wrong, we teach, when making such reasonable arguments. A premise may be dubious. Or the logical train from a premise to a conclusion may be faulty. In my view, Lewis' Trilemma suffers at least from the latter. Even if we grant the first and second premise (Jesus was not crazy; Jesus was not a fiend), there is no reason to believe that the only logical conclusion—based on the word "consequently"—is that he was and is God. There are other options (perhaps he was simply a great moral teacher as Lewis denies). In the composition course, I believe Lewis' Trilemma may serve as a good example of faulty reasoning as well as that questionable shift from faith to intellectual certainty that Dewey describes.

Apart from intellectual claims for the existence of God, however, Lewis' work can provide a wonderful example for students in the composition course. As Michael-John DePalma suggests, Lewis can help students invent "language resources that will provide the audience with an opportunity to connect to the sacred moments" that those students want to convey (237). By turning to Lewis' notion that our most profound experiences "cannot be communicated except by hints, similes, and metaphors," DePalma writes that it is in "this realm of discourse that we might look in the future to help religious students more effectively articulate their beliefs, commitments, and experiences" (237). In this particular realm, where students work to express and describe what religion has done for them/to them/around them, Lewis' work can in fact be a treasure trove.

Disassociating the metaphysical from religious belief—even within a carefully prescribed site like the composition classroom—is clearly no easy task. As James talks of our habitual native tendencies, Dewey too recognizes that "tradition and custom, especially when emotionally charged, are a part of the habits that have become one with our very being" (*Common* 15). Indeed, "the emotional deposit connected with prior teaching floods the whole situation" (13). But this is part of our work. When most of us teach writing today, we confront emotionally charged issues like race, class, gender, and sexual orientation on a regular basis. We've set our boundaries and mapped our approach, and we can do the same with religion.

To that end, a final word on experience, as this term is so central to all these pragmatists and so hard to pin down. Ultimately, Dewey emphasizes the "difference between an experience having a religious force because of what it does in and to the processes of living and religious experience as a separate kind of thing" (14). What we label as religious or religion can not be "marked off," he says, from all of our other experiences and activities "to validate a belief in some special kind of object and also to justify some special kind of practice" (10, 11). He adds too that not "all experiences are genuinely or equally educative," and that any particular "experience is mis-educative that has the effect of arresting or distorting the growth of further experience" (*Philosophy* 507). The value of experience is based in large part on whether it leads to "the possibilities of having richer experience in the future" (507), for "every experience lives on in further experiences" (508). But too often, Dewey says, the supernatural element of religion is so focused on justifying a preconceived notion from the past that such fresh experiences down the road get little attention.

John Dewey saw the possibility of religious belief as invaluable if freed from its metaphysical chains and understood as always directed at the terrestrial problems of living people. Understood as such, he unequivocally emphasized the importance of faith, for it encompasses "all that is significant in human experience" (*Common* 57).

Zen and the Art of Motorcycle Maintenance: *An Extended Example*

Phaedrus was having a hard time in his rhetoric class. His students weren't lazy. They tried, but they struggled to write. They were, as he put it, "very serious, disciplined, and hardworking," but lacking imagination (Pirsig 191). One particular student wanted to write an essay about the United States. Phaedrus suggested she just write about Bozeman, Montana, but that didn't work either, as she still didn't know where to begin. Finally, he told her, "Narrow it down to the *front* of *one* building on the main street of Bozeman. The Opera House. Start with the upper left-hand brick" (191).

She did, and it worked. She wrote all kinds of interesting stuff. Phaedrus thought a lot about why this worked, and he

> concluded she was evidently stopped with the same kind of blockage that had paralyzed him on his first day of teaching. She was blocked because she was trying to repeat, in her writing, things she had already heard, just as on the first day he had tried to repeat things he had already decided to say…. She was strangely unaware that she could look and see freshly for herself, as she wrote, without primary regard for what had been said before. The narrowing down to one brick destroyed the blockage because it was so obvious she *had* to do some original and direct seeing [192].

In other classes he explored this hypothesis by asking students to write about "the back of his thumb," or a coin. These worked as well. He found that once students "got into the idea of seeing directly for themselves they also saw there was no limit to the amount they could say. It was a confidence-building assignment, too, because what they wrote, even though seemingly trivial, was nevertheless their own thing, not a mimicking of someone else's" (192). Imitation has its value, Phaedrus knew, but too often it only blunts the imagination.

Phaedrus is the name that Robert Pirsig gives to the narrator's "prior" self, before electroshock therapy, in *Zen and the Art of Motorcycle Maintenance*. While wrestling with what qualifies as good writing in the classroom, Phaedrus is also concerned (or obsessed, really) with the broader idea of Quality—what it is, and how to define it. He decides, finally, that we cannot define it. If we try, we end up "defining something less than Quality itself" (255). Among the reasons he gives for this conclusion is that Quality is what prompts us to create our world in the first place: it is the "continuing stimulus which our environment puts upon us" to name our world and function within it. In other words, it is the source of everything, and we can't agree on a single definition "not because Quality is different, but because people are different in terms of experience" (254).

At one point, Pirsig turns to mathematics as an example, citing the work of Jules Henri Poincare (1854–1912). During Poincare's lifetime, Pirsig writes, the certainty of mathematics came into question. The field was confronted with conflicting truths. There were, as Pirsig puts it, "*two* contradictory visions of unshakable scientific truth, true for all men of all ages, regardless of their individual preferences" (267). The question that arose, of course, was which one is right? Poincare said that "we should first ask ourselves what is the nature of geometric axioms. Are they synthetic *a priori* judgments, as Kant said? That is, do they exist as a fixed part of man's consciousness, independently of experience and uncreated by experience?" (268). Poincare said no. If they were, then they would "impose themselves upon us with such force that we couldn't conceive the contrary proposition.... There would be no non–Euclidean geometry" (268).

To ask, then, whether this geometry or that geometry is "true" is to ask the wrong question. This question, in fact, "has no meaning. As well ask whether the metric system is true and the avoirdupois system is false; whether Cartesian coordinates are true and polar coordinates are false. One geometry cannot be more true than another; it can only be more *convenient*. Geometry is not true, it is advantageous" (269). Even in mathematics, there are no fixed laws that we must always refer to, or try to figure out. What we do is choose among the various possibilities in front of us and try to "eliminate the useless ones, or rather, to avoid the trouble of making them, and the rules that must guide the choice are extremely fine and delicate. It's almost impossible to state them precisely; they must be felt rather than formulated" (272). Which brings us back to Quality, and the idea that "you know what it is, yet you don't know what it is" (184). We're also reminded here of one of Pirsig's initial objectives in the book, which is "to see if in that strange separation of what man is from what man does we may have some clues as to what the hell has gone wrong in this twentieth century" (28).

In the United States, Pirsig became the most popular layman's philosopher of his time, and much of the pragmatic approach I describe in this book can be gleaned from his discussion of Quality outlined above. It's an approach that can help guide writers to that "upper left-hand brick" of religion—a fresh and focused look at what it does in the world, always contingent and contextual, and based on experience.

CHAPTER 3

God in the Comp Class: Boundaries and Places to Look

> There is an aspect of our vocation that is
> sacred … our work is not merely to share
> information but to share in the intellectual
> and spiritual growth of our students. To
> teach in a manner that respects and cares
> for the souls of our students is essential if
> we are to provide the necessary conditions
> where learning can most deeply and
> intimately begin.
> —bell hooks

> A poem, a stink, a grating noise, a quality
> of light, a tone, a habit, a nostalgia, a dream.
> Cannery Row is the gathered and scattered…
> —John Steinbeck

> I wish at the outset to clear myself of that
> confusion of religion with Veneration
> which enables most men to imagine themselves
> religious when they are only reverent.
> —Bernard Shaw

The epigraph above by hooks illustrates the daunting challenge teachers face in doing good work. Like Cannery Row, the sacred, the spiritual, and the "souls of our students" can be so many different slippery things at the very same time. The pragmatic distinction that Shaw makes between religious and reverent provides a direction for the first-year composition course that I want to flesh out a bit with some concrete examples. I began this book by referring to the first composition reader I ever taught (*Writing as Reflective Action* by Carter Duncan and Sherrie Gradin) and, more specifically, to an essay in it by John Updike that deals with religion. I want to look at that essay now through our pragmatic lens, but first a quick reminder on the general framework I've tried to outline so far.

Whether religion comes up by chance or design, we can highlight that verbal move I mentioned earlier, a move from "is" to "does," as a way to avoid the same ontological dead-ends we've run into for years. To explore and critique our notions of God, we look to our everyday experience, pull together the different things that religious belief "does" in the world, and then ask ourselves how it's useful. When we use the term "useful," we mean how religion helps (or doesn't help) to improve the human condition. This method is beholden to nothing other than sentient, terrestrial beings. It is meant to provide some boundaries for working with religion *as a social and political power* in the composition class. In his book *God: A Biography*, Jack Miles begins by saying, "I write here about the life of the Lord God as—and only as—the protagonist of a classic of world literature." He adds, "I do not attempt … to make an original statement about God as an extraliterary reality" (10), and that within the confines of his project, "knowledge of God as a literary character neither precludes nor requires belief in God" (4). In the comp class, we can proceed in a similar way by exploring the issue of religious belief as—*and only as*—a social and political force worthy of our attention in this particular classroom. We might add, too, that our exploration does not require or preclude "belief in God."

Back, now, to John Updike. Religion is a central theme in much of Updike's writing, and the ground from which he worked when it came to this topic is worth some discussion. Throughout his career, Updike relied heavily upon the thinking of the Danish writer Soren Kierkegaard and the German theologian Karl Barth. More specifically, as Marshall Boswell notes in describing Updike's early existential crisis, the two books that "saved him from this abyss" were *Fear and Trembling* (1843) by Kierkegaard and *The Word of God and the Word of Man* (1928) by Barth (43). As Boswell suggests, what drew Updike to these authors and these works in particular was the way in which they employed a "dialectical approach to religious issues in which defining oppositions do not resolve into a satisfying synthesis but rather remain in sustained tension and ambiguity" (43). As Updike has said himself, "My books attempt to show the several sides of something, and leave the reader with the awareness of a difficulty, rather than with the grasping of a slogan or a motto to live by" (*Conversations* 50). In other words, Updike wasn't trying to lead his readers to any particular conclusion; he wanted his readers to grapple productively, and continuously, with religious belief.

In setting up this dynamic, Updike often drew upon many of "Barth's central tenets, particularly that which insists on a simple, uncompromising faith in the existence of God" (Wagner 61). But His existence "is manifest not by rational processes"; it is a faith that "cannot be achieved through man's reason or understanding" (61). Boswell argues that Barth's God is, in fact, Updike's God, a God that we simply cannot know as human beings. "There is no way from us to God," Barth writes in *The Word of God and the Word of Man*, "not even *via negativa*—not even *via dialectica* nor *paradoxa*. The god who stood at the end of some human way ... would not be God" (177). Barth's theology, then, rests in part on the idea that God is something Wholly Other than us, something we cannot comprehend. So too for John Updike. When it comes to God, "the debate, as in all of Updike's best work, remains in the end open, dynamic, still restlessly in play" (Boswell 56).

Insomuch as God's existence is beyond the reach of human reason, Updike tends to circumvent that question altogether, and focus rather on religion as a social force in the lives of everyday people. We can see this approach in the essay that I ran away from my first semester teaching, "On Being a Self Forever." Here, we are prompted to kick around the idea of an afterlife, and how that idea helps us to reflect upon who we are. We are not encouraged to come to any conclusion about the truth of an afterlife, but instead to think about questions like how does belief in an afterlife help us contemplate our individual selves, and how does it help us to understand these selves in relation to others? And, practically speaking, is an afterlife something we would even want, "this self, these scattered fingerprints on the air, to persist forever, to outlast the atomic universe?" (Duncan and Gradin 24). We're meant to question as well whether contemplating this at all is a waste of time:

> Ridiculous, excessive, unreasonable, you say? No more, the response must be, than existence as it is, than the worlds that are, with trees and flowers, ocean and sky, stars and stones, animals and insects and men. Our self is thrust into a manifold reality that is thoroughly gratuitous, and the faith in an afterlife, however much our reason ridicules it,

very modestly extends our faith that each moment of our consciousness will be followed by another—that a coherent matrix has been prepared for this precious self of ours. The guarantee that our self enjoys
an intended relation to the outer world is most, if not all, of what we
ask from religion [26].

The notion of an afterlife affects how we see ourselves and how we
conduct ourselves in the present world we need to share. Referring to Unamuno's observation that "consciousness is a disease," Updike writes that
"religion would relieve the symptoms" (32). He is referring to both a religious attitude, free from a supernatural deity as John Dewy describes it, as
well as to the various historic institutions: "Religion construed, of course,
broadly, not only in the form of the world's barbaric and atrocious religious
orthodoxies but in the form of any private system, be it adoration of Elvis
Presley or hatred of nuclear weapons, be it fetishism of politics or popular
culture" (32). He notes "How remarkably fertile the religious imagination
is," and suggests that "falling in love—its mythologization of the beloved
and everything that touches her or him—is an invented religion,

> and religious also is our persistence, against all the powerful post-
> Copernican, post–Darwinian evidence that we are insignificant acci-
> dents within a vast uncaused churning, in feeling that our life is a
> story, with a pattern and a moral and an inevitability—that, as Emer-
> son said, "a thread runs through all things: all worlds are strung on it,
> as beads: and men, and events, and life, come to us, only because of
> that thread." That our subjectivity, in other words, dominates, through
> secret channels, outer reality, and the universe has a personal structure
> [32–33].

With passages like this we can lead our students to consider the different
ways religion, "broadly" defined, as Updike puts it, is set to use in the
world. What are the consequences for community that may result from
religious belief as he describes it? Updike adds that "religion enables us
to ignore nothingness and get on with the jobs of life" (34). If this is
true, how so? If not, why not?

In contemplating the three dominate prophetic religions of today,
he writes,

> How gorgeously strange the religions of others seem! The world's
> outstanding believers these days are the Moslems: what forms has
> God taken in their heads—what does Allah mean to them as they

66

surge forward in their Iranian human waves or Palestinian suicide missions? What common image animates all these close-packed male bodies bowing in unison on some dusty equatorial *masjid?* It is not the Christian God—or gods, for out of Paraguayan Catholics, Vermont Congregationalists, Utah Mormons, and New Zealand Anglicans sprout as many gods as are carved on a Jain temple wall. The Jewish God, as best He can be glimpsed in the United States, wears yet a different face. He seems meatier, more unbuttoned than His Christian offspring; He does not excite the churchgoer's anxious either/or, that "Does He?" or "Doesn't He?" in regard to His existence, that angst-generating crux of faith. Christianity has somehow taken hold of religion at the wrong end of the stick—the inhuman, or wholly other, end. The Jewish attitude seems in comparison humorous and submissive: it's His choice, to exist or not [33].

There is a strong pragmatic bend to this passage—a bend toward focusing on the actions and lived-experience of human beings when it comes to religion. God's existence is not the question, but rather how belief in Him "animates" and "excites" believers on the ground. In reference to Christianity, the phrase "wholly other" invokes Karl Barth, and provides a lead for us in the writing class to be clear that any focus on the "inhuman" is a focus on "the wrong end of the stick."

When writing earlier about Dewey and C. S. Lewis I talked about the making of reasonable, intellectual deductions with respect to religious belief. In describing his attempt at coming to God, Updike offers his own: "Early in my adolescence, trapped within the airtight case for atheism, I made this logical formulation: 1. If God does not exist, the world is a horror-show. 2. The world is not a horror show. 3. Therefore, God exists" (34). He recognizes that the "second premise, of course, is the weaker," and implies that the first premise may stand on shaky legs of its own (34–35). This was not the route he took. He found real Christianity to be vague and impossible to grasp intellectually, and it seems that that obscurity is what helped him to find it: "Though signs of belief (churches, public prayers, mottos on coins) existed everywhere, when you moved toward Christianity it disappeared, as fog solidly opaque in the distance thins to transparency when you walk into it. I decided I nevertheless *would* believe" (35). He credits "a few authors, a very few—Chesterton, Eliot, Unamuno, Kierkegaard, Karl Barth—who helped me believe" (35). In these writers, he saw that "God is the God of the living"

(35), not of the dead, or of heaven or hell or anything that happens in a wholly other place. And he adds that what religion did for him was push him to write: "What small faith I have has given me what artistic courage I have" (35).

What does it press us to do, and what does it do for us on this human stage? These are the sorts of questions this essay seems to ask, and a variety of answers are offered throughout. He suggests, for instance, that "one believes not merely to dismiss from one's life a degrading and immobilizing fear of death but to possess that Archimedean point outside the world from which to move the world" (36). There is also the profound issue of loneliness: "religion tries to put us at ease in this world. Being human cannot be borne alone. We need other presences" (37). And, to put it bluntly, the author admits that "Christianity gave me something to write about, and a semblance of a backbone, and a place to go Sunday mornings" (37).

By the end of the essay there is a strong sense that we cannot say anything for certain about the reality of God. Truth may be something to strive for, but it can't quite ever be caught. As Updike says in conclusion, "What I have written here strains to be true but nevertheless is not true *enough*" (38). Even though it may leave us restless and uncomfortable, our best bet is to explore the influence religious belief has on our actions and how we're inclined to put it to use. Advice perhaps captured in a final description of the author's childhood home to which he has returned as an adult. In the room where he slept, a room he was intimately familiar with, he notices that "a felt piece of local kitsch I always disliked has been taken down. It showed an Amish man standing erect with a hammer and a carpenter's square, above the slogan WHAT A MAN DOES, THAT HE IS. I believe it, but didn't like reading it" (39). If I were to teach this essay today, I might end by asking my students why they think he believed this slogan, and why he didn't like reading it.

In chapter 4 I look at a number of texts in some detail, but I want to talk here about one other essay that may help to find our focus and set some boundaries. The essay is "The Marginal World" by Rachel Carson. We might simply start with the title, and encourage students to consider the word "marginal" as Carson intends it—not in terms of being insignificant, but in terms of connecting, being in between, or on the edge of something that leads to something else.

With our approach to religious belief in mind, we can ask students to consider the following quote from the opening paragraph: "Today a little more land may belong to the sea, tomorrow a little less. Always the edge of the sea remains an elusive and indefinable boundary" (214). The shore, as she describes it, is a place of possibility, not certainty. It "is a world that keeps alive the sense of continuing creation and of the relentless drive of life. Each time I enter it, I gain some new awareness of its beauty and its deeper meanings, sensing that intricate fabric by which one creature is linked with another, and each with its surroundings" (215).

Carson describes a little pool in a cave that can be seen "only rarely and briefly when the lowest of the year's low tides fall below it" (215). It is a magical place, and she seems to describe it in both theological as well as evolutionary terms. The former can be seen in the following passage, which invokes the hand of God creating us in His own image and our brief time on this planet as corporeal beings:

> In the moment when I looked into the cave a little elfin starfish hung down, suspended by the merest thread.... It reached down to touch its own reflection, so perfectly delineated that there might have been, not one starfish, but two. The beauty of the reflected images and of the limpid pool itself was the poignant beauty of things that are ephemeral, existing only until the sea should return to fill the little cave [216].

This "fairy cave," however, that includes "creatures so exquisitely fashioned that they seemed unreal" (216), may also be read in a Darwinian light, "where the forces of evolution are at work today" (219) and where "every detail was functionally useful, every stalk and hydranth and petal-like tentacle fashioned for dealing with the realities of existence" (216).

Throughout the essay, Carson weaves together words that are too often seen as antonyms—"revelation" and "creation" together with "evolution." It takes all of these, a reader may conclude, not one in and of itself to fashion the mysterious, beautiful world she describes. "Marginal" in this sense becomes a meeting place where, literally, spectacular things happen. Here is a metaphor we can press in the composition class— spectacular things can happen in those "marginal places" where a kind of ongoing negotiation, or mediation, occurs between land and sea.

Mediation is, in fact, a key term for us to consider when it comes to pragmatism. Mediation is not compromise in the sense of appease-ment, in the sense that each side "gives in" a little bit: we'll grant you this (although we're not happy about it) if you'll grant us that. Here you often end up with a watered down version of what you had before. In, for example, Noah Feldman's book *Divided by God*, Feldman suggests the following to mend this division in the United States. For atheists, we would cease, unequivocally, any federal funding of religion (no more school vouchers, faith-based initiatives, etc.). For theists, we would allow overt displays of religious belief on public ground, on our money, in speeches by our presidents, etc. But as well intentioned as this compro-mise may be, it is unlikely to work because it is just that—a tenuous compromise that leaves us in the same basic place with the same basic problem. In contrast, mediation starts on a fresh field by sidestepping worn, confrontational, two-dimensional tracks to move in a third direc-tion altogether. Our focus on usefulness as social responsibility sets us in motion; it does so, first of all, by forcing each side to recognize that the other may have a point. In other words, we don't start by giving something up, we start by gaining something we didn't see before. From there, we can begin to "mediate and bring into relationship" our oppos-ing ideas (Roskelly and Ronald 83), with the intermediate, controlling agent being our shared responsibility to one another. But this takes, of course, collaboration and hard work.

Avoiding the Ontological

The strong sense of contingency that comes from our focus on lived experience should swing us away from ontological claims about religion. But this is worth talking about in more detail. No matter what we assign in the writing class—from readings and informal writing like journal entries to more formal writing like research papers—we can work to steer students away from ontological arguments. If, for instance, a stu-dent is writing an argumentative paper on religion, we can make clear that positions should not be rooted in essential, a priori claims. In the comp class, when we work with racism, sexism, classism, and homo-phobia to prompt students to think and write about the world in which they live, we look at what those things have done in the world, and we move in one direction. We know where we're going, and we're ok with ontological arguments: we have seen what misogyny does, and based on that, we have decided what it is. As I noted in the introduction to this book, the case is different with religion.

Asking students to write out a syllogism for their overall argument can help keep them on track. If any part of that syllogism makes a metaphysical or ontological claim, it's probably not going to work for us. For instance, if a student writes a paper arguing that the Boy Scouts of America can exclude atheists, a syllogism that would work might go something like this: (1) Private institutions in the United States may exclude those whose views are inconsistent with the institution's mission. (2) The Boy Scouts of America is a private institution in the United States. (3) Therefore, the Boy Scouts of America may exclude those whose views are inconsistent with its mission. One that won't fly would sound something like this: (1) As a Christian institution, the Boy Scouts of America teaches moral values. (2) Atheists do not hold moral values. (3) Therefore, The Boy Scouts of America may exclude atheists.

For most of us, ontological tendencies come naturally. We like the essence of things, we like simple, yes or no, true or untrue. As Stephen Jay Gould notes, "Our minds tend to work by dichotomy—that is, by conceptualizing complex issues as 'either/or' pairs, dictating a choice of one extreme or other, with no middle ground (or golden mean) available for any alternative resolution" (50). Gould speculates that maybe our "tendency to dichotomize represents some powerful baggage from an evolutionary past, when limited consciousness could not transcend 'on or off,' 'yes or no,' 'fight or flee,' 'move or rest'—and the neurology of simpler brains became wired in accordance with such exigencies" (51). Whatever the reason, it does seem that most of us are inclined to see one of only two rather bright, simple answers when it comes to a number of topics. Finding incentive to work on different ground doesn't come easy. As we're learning, however, searching for such ground is a healthy thing to do in more ways than one.

For example, in her article entitled "How to Train the Aging Brain," Barbara Strauch describes how looking at the world from a different point of view becomes vital for our mental health. Citing professor Kathleen Taylor, she notes that "the brain is plastic and continues to change" in the sense of "allowing for greater complexity and deeper understanding," and she adds that "for adults, one way to nudge neurons in the right direction is to challenge the very assumptions they have worked so hard to accumulate while young. With a brain already full of well-connected pathways, adult learners should 'jiggle their synapses a bit' by confronting thoughts that are contrary to their own" (2). Addressing adult education in particular, Strauch says that simply learning new facts doesn't help us much: "continued brain development and a richer form of learning may require that you 'bump up against people and ideas' that are different" (2). As Dr. Taylor adds, "There's a place for information.... We need to know stuff. But we need to move beyond that and challenge our perception of the world" (2). In other words, we need to startle our "established brain connections" by entertaining points of view we are not in the habit of holding.

Such "stretching," as Strauch puts it, can take the form of anything from "learning a foreign language to taking a different route to work" (2). In referring to Dr. Jack Mezirow, she adds that "adults learn best if presented with what he calls a 'disorienting dilemma,' or something that 'helps you critically reflect on the assumptions you've acquired'" (3). Dr. Mezirow came up with this approach "30 years ago after he studied women who had gone back to school. The women took this bold step only after having many conversations that helped them 'challenge their own ingrained perceptions of that time when women could not do what men could do'" (3). Stretching in this regard is a principle point of higher education, of course, and certainly a component of the composition course. We can put it to use when facing religious belief.

The Double-Entry Journal

This section may just as well belong in chapter 4 with other assignments, but I include it here to help us map our approach. Over the years I've asked students to write in their journals about one example of how religion affects our lives in the world. It could be almost anything, but it must be a tangible example of what religious belief *does* for us. It could come from first-hand experience, from the news, from stories they have heard, etc. This journal is based on Ann Berthoff's Double-Entry approach. The idea is to write down their initial responses and opinions on the left-hand page of their notebook. They shouldn't look at it again until they come to the next class, where we take ten minutes or so for them to respond to that initial observation on the opposite, right-hand page. As Berthoff explains, the opposing pages are in direct dialogue with each other—their thinking, and then their thinking about their thinking. The point is to help students face their own engrained inclinations, or in Berthoff's words, to "conduct [a] 'continuing audit of meaning' that is at the heart of learning to read and write critically" (45). It's designed, again as Berthoff puts it, "to encourage [them] to look and look again" (46); in our case, to look and look again at their beliefs about the usefulness of religion. In short, I tell them, "when you find something, just write what you think. Then later, respond to what you thought."

When I was teaching in Chile, religious belief came up now and then in their journals even when I didn't assign it. Chile is a very Catholic country—divorce has been legal for only a decade—and while many students don't appear to think much about it, religion is often there. One of the journal entries, I remember, focused on the small but powerful influence of creationism in Chilean culture. She referred to an article that I had given them: In "Evolution's Bottom Line," Holden Thorp argues that theories of creationism and intelligent design not only hinder our ability to improve our general condition, but they also hurt America's ability to compete in the global marketplace. He writes that "both sides say they are fighting for lofty goals and defending the truth. But lost in all this truth-defending are more pragmatic issues that have to do with the young people whose educations are at stake here and this pesky fact: creationism has no commercial application. Evolution does" (A27). He goes on to suggest that "the battle is about more than which truth is truthier, it's about who will be allowed to innovate and where they will do it" (A27). This applies to *us*, my student wrote. We're a small country. And we're pretty far away from everything. If we want to work with the rest of the world, if we want to grow as a country, we have to compete. We need religion, but we can't have one that "holds us back."

Another student wrote in his journal about the archbishop of Santiago, Francisco Javier Errázuriz. During the elections of 2005, when Michelle Bachelet's opponent Sebastian Piñera started running ads saying that Bachelet (like Ricardo Lagos before her) was "godless," Bishop

Errázuriz made a very public speech condemning such tactics. God is not to be wielded as a political weapon, he said. That's not how He fits into the equation. I learned a lot from their journals, actually. There were some especially powerful descriptions of the good and the bad that the church, in its various forms, did during the reign of Pinochet. Most entries depicted a church that "did good," to say the least (I was struck by how many of my students had relatives or friends of the family imprisoned, tortured, or murdered). Through their journals I also began to discover the "formal" class structure that exists just below the surface. There is, apparently, a real scale—A, B, C1, C2, C3, D, and E—which is used for everything from job and loan applications to dinner reservations and taxi service (you also can't apply for most jobs without attaching a photo to your application). Your "place" is assigned not just according to the money you have, but to your last name, where you live, where you went to high school, etc. (We, of course, don't discriminate like this in the States.) A few of my students wrote about how their church in particular or religion in general helped to dispel or perpetuate this system. Overall, their journal entries were strong (often stronger than their papers). For this, I have Ann Berthoff to thank.

Separation of Church and State

Most students have heard of the phrase "separation of church and state." Often, however, when it comes up in their writing, or if we get in to a real discussion about it, not many know where this phrase actually comes from or how it has been interpreted over the years. This can be a fruitful place for us to go in the composition class.

In the First Amendment to the Constitution, there are two clauses regarding religion. They read, "Congress shall make no law respecting an establishment of religion, or prohibiting the free exercise thereof." On their face, they sound straightforward; they have, however, proven to be anything but. For starters, we know that those who wrote and revised them didn't agree on exactly what they meant. They have also been seen as standing in contradiction to one another. For instance, the Supreme Court has heard a number of cases on whether or not a state can offer scholarships to clerical students. If it does, is it helping to "establish" religion? And if it doesn't offer scholarships to only those students, is it infringing on their right to freely exercise their religious beliefs? The Court has settled on the general notion that the government must remain "neutral" when addressing religion (see, for instance, *Employment Division, Department of Human Resources of Oregon v. Smith*, 1990). But that of course leads to a new round of questions and problems.

In class, I've asked my students to play around a little with these clauses, to look at the grammatical structure (is it significant that the first is an independent clause and the second a dependent clause; does there appear to be more emphasis on the first clause because of its position and structure?) and to think about some of the bigger questions that they generate. For example, in the 1971 case *Lemmon v. Kurtzman*, the Court laid out a three-part test to determine if the government had taken a neutral stand with respect to religion. This test states that the law or action in question must have a secular purpose, its principle result may not promote or hinder religious belief, and it cannot prompt "excessive government entanglement" with religion. Without too much more information, I've asked students to think and write informally about this test. Does it seem reasonable off the bat? How might it help clarify those original Constitutional clauses? Does it create additional problems or questions? If so, what might they be? (It may, in addition, be worth pointing out that the Constitution itself is a wonderful example of revision and contingency—from 1791 to 1992, it has been amended 27 times.)

These musings could lead to a more substantial paper assignment, where students begin with those "simple" clauses in the First Amendment (or even just one of them), outline what some of the more important Supreme Court cases have held on the issue, and then enter the conversation themselves by making an original argument. Most cases involve one clause or the other: those that involve the "establishment clause" usually revolve around religious belief and schools or public displays of religion on government grounds. The "free exercise clause" has also involved schools, but tends as well to include employment, business, and tax issues. With respect to both clauses, there has long been the question of what constitutes "religion" in the first place. The Court has said it is not necessary that an individual belong to a particular faith or sect; the question is how meaningful and paramount the belief is in the life of that individual (see *Welsh v. United States*). Such language can provide a great deal of room for debate, imagination, and writing in the composition course.

Students don't have to look long to find contemporary examples of these questions across the country. A number of states have recently seen battles inside various courthouses over the public display of religious tenets on government ground. Lawyers in Ohio, Kentucky, and Pennsylvania have also recently fought over the proper place of creationism (or intelligent design) and Darwin's theory of evolution in the curriculums of public schools. Many of these cases, which have yet to be argued, can be said to have their roots in the *State of Tennessee v. John Thomas Scopes* (1925). Often called the Monkey Trial, Scopes was tried and convicted for breaking a Tennessee law which made it illegal to teach evolution at public schools within the state. Almost a century later, courts across the land have found themselves hearing one echo or another of this famous trial.

In January 2012, the U.S. Supreme Court handed down what has been called a landmark case with respect to religious freedom and the First Amendment. In *Hosanna-Tabor Evangelical Lutheran Church and School v. EEOC*, the plaintiff claimed her employer violated a federal anti-discrimination law when it fired her (specifically, she claimed that it violated the Americans with Disabilities Act when it let her go after she started to struggle with narcolepsy). On appeal, the Supreme Court held that federal anti-discrimination laws do not apply when it comes to employment issues between religious institutions and their ministers. The Court based its reasoning on the First Amendment, saying that both the Establishment clause and the Free Exercise clause do indeed effectively create a "ministerial exception": the state cannot interfere with how religious institutions make decisions about the hiring and firing of their ministers. Chief Justice Roberts, who wrote the unanimous opinion, argued the following:

> Requiring a church to accept or retain an unwanted minister, or punishing a church for failing to do so, intrudes upon more than a mere employment decision. Such action interferes with the internal governance of the church, depriving the church control over the selection of those who will personify its beliefs. By imposing an unwanted minis-

ter, the state infringes the Free Exercise Clause, which protects a religious group's right to shape its own faith and mission through its appointments. According the state the power to determine which individuals will minister to the faithful also violates the Establishment Clause, which prohibits government involvement in such ecclesiastical decisions [*Hosanna*].

Hosanna has been read as a huge victory for religious freedom in this country. It also opens up a number of interesting questions for us to grapple with in the writing class. Is the Court's decision a reasonable reading of the First Amendment? In what other institutions or processes might we apply the Court's reasoning—i.e., where might we carve out other exemptions like the "ministerial exemption" with respect to religious freedom and the First Amendment? What might be some of the consequences of allowing churches or church-related schools to operate outside federal anti-discrimination laws? Or, what are church administrators now free to do? Who qualifies as a minister? If the government should not meddle in the internal affairs of religious institutions, how should we police the way in which religious institutions influence the internal affairs of our various branches of government? How is this ruling in keeping with the "property tax exemption" granted religious institutions, or the Court's finding that religious publications are not exempt from state sales taxes? And, back to an old question, what qualifies as a religious institution? These are just a few of the difficult questions that we might consider when writing about this case and the separation of church and state clauses found in the First Amendment.

When talking about the separation of church and state in the U.S., it might also be useful to consider Roger Williams. Williams fled England where he and others were persecuted for having religious beliefs that didn't line up with those of the king—at that time in Great Britain, church and state were a single entity. What he found in Puritan Massachusetts, however, was more of the same. In the New World of John Winthrop, Williams was tried and eventually exiled. As a result, he founded Rhode Island, "the first place in the Western world where people could believe in any God they wished—or no God at all—without fear of retribution" (Nocera 1).

As Timothy Egan notes in his article "Theocracy and Its Discontents," the Bay Colony was certainly not the only place in the New World where God's law was the unyielding law of the land. "The Mormons," he writes, "for all the cheery optimism of their present state, were birthed in brutal theocracy, first in Nauvoo, Illinois, and later in the State of Deseret, as their settlement in present-day Utah was called." The U.S. Constitution, which separated "church from state, press from government, had no place [in their view] ... it took a threat to march the United States Army out to the rogue settlement around the Great Salt Lake to persuade Mormon leaders that their control did not extend beyond matters of the soul" (2). Citing John Barry, Egan writes that Roger Williams "believed that humans, being imperfect, would inevitably err in applying God's laws," and that, indeed, "Forced worship stinks in God's nostrils" (2). Williams was by no means an atheist, but he wanted to stop the way in which God's law was enforced by errant humans here on earth.

Joe Nocera, Timothy Egan, John Barry and others writing in 2012 have pointed to Roger Williams in response to Rick Santorum's presidential bid of the same year. Barry, in fact, has said that "Rick Santorum is John Winthrop" (Nocera 1). Nocera writes that Santorum is the "standard bearer" for the "many Americans [who] do not readily accept" that state and church should in no way inform one another. Santorum has said that "laws cannot be neutral. There is only moral or immoral" (2), and he has said that Barack Obama holds a "phony theology," one based not on the Bible and therefore un–American. Santorum has also argued that climate change is a hoax, reminding us that "we are put on this earth as creatures of God to have dominion over the earth," and he has, in Egan's words, "long tried to get his Biblical principles taught to children in public schools—insisting that 'creationism' should be in every American classroom, and trying to enforce that through riders to education bills when he was a senator" (3). Santorum received such attention because he not only survived into March as the only real challenger to Mitt Romney for the Republican nomination, but amassed a following that could have pushed him over the top.

Santorum's popularity might be surprising given the political platform from which he launched his presidential campaign. In Pennsylvania in 2006, he lost his bid to keep his seat in the Senate by one of the widest margins in Senate history. But his extremely conservative opinions on social issues and the emphasis he places on the fact that those opinions come from his faith appeal to a huge swath of the country.

Sean Reilly, one of Santorum's aids who now works as a political consultant, has said that "Rick Santorum is a Catholic missionary.... That's what he is. He's a Catholic missionary who happens to be in the Senate" (Sokolove 58). There is little doubt that he is on a mission. As Senator Susan Collins notes, "He believes there should be more of an intertwining of government and religion, and he believes it passionately" (61). Over the years, Santorum has consistently argued that "to completely separate moral views from public life ... is a dangerous thing" (61). "How is it possible," he asks, "to believe in the existence of God yet refuse to express outrage when his moral code is flouted? How is it possible that there exists so little space in the public square for the standards that follow from belief in a transcendent God?" (61).

In February 2012, Santorum expressed these beliefs again when he said that John F. Kennedy's speech in 1960 on the intermingling of government and religion made him want to "throw up." In his speech, Kennedy said, "I believe in an America where the separation of church and state is absolute" (2). As a Catholic, Kennedy wanted to let voters know that if elected, he would not be looking to the Vatican when making presidential decisions (he was also trying to avoid what happened to Al Smith some thirty years earlier—Smith was a Catholic presidential candidate who lost in a landslide to Herbert Hoover in large part because of an unrelenting and brutal media attack from Protestants who claimed that Smith would, in fact, turn the United States into a voice for the Vatican). In his article "The View from Bay Ridge, 1960," Gerald Howard writes that with this speech, "Kennedy didn't just disarm a ticking bomb that would have derailed his campaign; he provided a template for dealing with one of the trickiest issues in American governance, the proper coexistence of church and state. For more than 50 years that speech has stood as the essential guiding statement of right thinking on this matter" (2). For many, John F. Kennedy was arguing for balance and tolerance, not for the exclusion of religious belief from the public sphere.

Santorum reads the speech differently, and his reading is by no means extraordinary. It didn't take long, of course, for him to hear that wanting to vomit was not an appropriate response to Kennedy's speech, and that he should reread the First Amendment of the Constitution, especially those two clauses about religion. On his behalf, however, came a number of different reactions, including an article titled, "Rick Santorum

Isn't Crazy" by Stanley Fish. Fish writes that if the Constitution calls for a separation of church and state, then "a number of Supreme Court justices and A-list legal academics have somehow missed the message" (3). He cites, for instance, *Wallace v. Jaffree* (1985), in which "Justice William Rehnquist called the 'wall of separation' a 'metaphor based on bad history, a metaphor which has proved useless as a guide to judging' and 'should be frankly and explicitly abandoned.'" There is also Justice Potter Stewart who often observed "that decisions based on a doctrine of strict separation display a hostility to religion and threaten to establish a 'religion of secularism.'" Stewart liked to cite Justice William O. Douglas, who noted in *Zorach v. Clauson* (1952) that "we are a religious people whose institutions presuppose a supreme being." Fish goes on to list a number of other Supreme Court justices who have held similar views, including Warren E. Burger, Byron White, Clarence Thomas, and Antonin Scalia (3).

Fish also refers to a number of legal academics, many of whom, he adds, worked as lawyers and/or served as judges at the federal level. For example, Michael McConnell from Stanford has argued that the separation of church and state is a "'narrow ideological position of the secular elite,' a position that 'relegates the large majority of the American public … to second-class citizenship.'" In addition to McConnell, Fish includes the following:

> Stephen Carter of Yale Law School, Douglas Laycock of the University of Virginia School of Law, Philip Hamburger of Columbia Law School, Michael Perry of Emory University School of Law, Frederick Mark Gedicks of Brigham Young's J. Reuben Clark Law School, Steven Smith of the law school at University of San Diego, Jeff Powell of the Duke University Law School and the late Richard John Neuhaus, author of "The Naked Public Square," are just a few of the many who have argued that the wall of separation thesis is historically, morally and politically indefensible [4].

To be clear, at the end of this list Fish writes, in parentheses, "I neither join nor dissent from this argument; I merely point out how widespread and respectable it is" (4). He takes pains to say that he is not suggesting Santorum is right, and he adds that the ex-senator's word choice is not always the greatest. But Santorum's central argument, Fish says, is not out of the loop.

Other Places to Look

Our culture is so imbued with religious belief that the reader doesn't need me to provide places to look for our purposes in the composition class. Nonetheless, my hope is that it's helpful to share here some particular prompts I have used in the past.

Several years ago I gave my first-year composition students the following prompt as a possible debate topic:

> The *Los Angeles Times* reports that "about two thirds of U.S medical schools now offer some form of training on the role of religion and spirituality in medicine." The same article notes that "Walter Larimore, an award-winning physician ... has declared that excluding God from a consultation should be grounds for malpractice" [Sloan A13]. Should medical schools offer this training, and should we heed Dr. Larimore's directive?

This sort of question has been around for some time, and it has produced some interesting answers. In "The Biology of Belief," Jeffrey Kluger writes that "atheists and believers may argue about religion, but one thing seems clear: having faith can improve your health. The next debate is inevitable: Why?" (122). Kluger begins by noting that "a growing body of scientific evidence suggests that faith may indeed bring us health" (122). He goes on to say that people

> who attend religious services do have a lower risk of dying in any given year than people who don't attend. People who believe in a loving God fare better after a diagnosis of illness than people who believe in a punitive God. No less a killer than AIDS will back off at least a bit when it's hit with a double-barreled blast of belief. "Even accounting for medications," says Dr. Gail Ironson, a professor of psychiatry and psychology at the University of Miami who studies HIV and religious belief, "spirituality predicts for better disease control" [122].

There are a number of doctors and specialists who argue that such conclusions can be easily accounted for with biological and empirical explanations. Dr. Richard Sloan, for example, does just that in his book *Blind Faith: The Unholy Alliance of Religion and Medicine.* Sloan says that science and religious belief simply don't mix—they work in different realms. But more and more scholars tend to agree with Kluger. Robert Hummer, a social demographer from the University of Texas, has been

81

studying a group of people since 1992. He has found that those "who never attend religious services have twice the risk of dying over the next eight years as people who attend once a week. People who fall somewhere between no churchgoing and weekly churchgoing also fall between in terms of mortality" (Kluger 125). And Hummer adds that people "embedded in religious communities are more likely to rely on one another for friendship, support, rides to doctor's appointments," etc. As a consequence, loneliness becomes less of a threat.

There are, in fact, many examples that highlight the advantages of religious belief when it comes to health issues: the intricate history of African American churches, the huge percentage of patients who say they would like their doctors to discuss their "religious needs ... and include a pastor in the mix if that would help" (126), and, more specifically, places like the Health Care Chaplaincy, "an organization of Christian, Jewish, Muslim, and Zen Buddhist board-certified chaplains affiliated with more than a dozen hospitals and clinics in the New York City area" (127). Much as William James would have said, Jeffrey Kluger concludes that while religious belief is certainly no replacement for science and medicine, "we can't afford to be choosy about where we look for answers. Doctors, patients, and pastors battling disease already know that help comes in a whole lot of forms. It's the result, not the source, that counts the most" (127).

A group of women who live in the Appalachian mountains might very well agree with Kluger's conclusion. In her book *A Communion of Friendship: Literacy, Spiritual Practice, and Women in Recovery*, Beth Daniell describes six women who work to develop a spiritual strength from reading, writing, and Al-Anon as they struggle to cope with husbands who are alcoholics. Of the twelve steps of Al-Anon, nine specifically reference God or call upon His help. For example, #3) "Made a decision to turn our will and lives over to the care of God *as we understood Him*"; #5) Admitted to God, to ourselves, and to another human being the exact nature of our wrongs"; #6) Were entirely ready to have God remove all these defects of character"; #7) Humbly asked Him to remove our shortcomings" (Daniell 171). As a program, however, Al-Anon does not discriminate based upon one's faith, belief, or spiritual orientation. Its doors are open to all who need its support.

Part of Daniell's project uncovers the way in which writing has helped a number of the women she worked with. She points, for instance, to Jennie, who "uses her God Can notes. This practice started for Jennie with an actual can in her kitchen—Folger's coffee, I think—that had pasted on it a label declaring "I Can't. God Can" (58). As Jennie explained,

> Some people can visualize putting people in God's hands, and that does it for them. Well, it doesn't do it for me. I have to write it down and put it in my God Can to get rid of it. I try to condense it into as few words as possible, a tiny slip of paper. It may be an inch or two inches long—I have one that's probably about three inches long, about half an inch wide. Now I have two God cans. One is actually a mahogany butterfly someone gave me [58–59].

Another woman, Judy, adds, "There is a release when I write and put it in my God Can. It seems more concrete. So when I have a real difficult time, then I write my prayers.... I have written things, pages, and folded them up and put the pages in the God Can. It's almost like a catharsis" (59).

Daniell outlines the way in which spirituality, coupled with reading and writing, can make such a positive impact in people's lives—or in this particular case, in women's well-being. Al-Anon provided an original spark for these women to communicate with each other and work on their common struggle.

As I was working on this chapter, I saw an interesting ad in a newspaper that may also provide a productive place for us to go in the comp class. The Boy Scouts of America (BSA) recently reconsidered its membership policy regarding homosexuals, and just after they did so the Freedom from Religion Foundation (FFRF) sponsored an ad that depicts a boy in a Boy Scout uniform pointing to the medals on his chest and saying, "This one's for swimming, this one's for woodcraft, this one's for religious bigotry..." (Freedom). Below this illustration, the ad congratulates the Boy Scouts for "lifting its longstanding, hurtful ban against gay membership" and asks the following question: "But why hasn't BSA stopped excluding nonreligious boys, too?" (Freedom).

The ad goes on to say, "BSA advertises, 'any boy may join,' yet explicitly bans atheists, nonbelievers and youngsters from nonreligious homes. BSA proudly excludes and stigmatizes the one in three young persons today who now identifies as nonreligious (Pew Survey, Oct. 9,

2012).″ It notes as well that "BSA's membership form contains a religious litmus test that defames freethinkers: 'The Boy Scouts of America maintain that no member can grow into the best kind of citizen without recognizing his obligation to God'" (Freedom). After these statements, the ad offers the following commentary:

> No one can grow into the best kind of citizen who discriminates against the nonreligious. It's what you do—not what you believe—that makes you a good person and a good citizen. BSA's vaunted "duty to God" has led it to cruelly place dogma over its duty to children. The intellectual rejection of claims for which there is no evidence is not only respectable, but vital to progress. What should not be respectable is treating any American, whether young or old, as a second-class citizen [Freedom].

The ad then invites readers to join the FFRF, which describes itself as devoted to "educating about nontheism, and keeping religion out of government" (Freedom).

With its reference to government, this ad, and the FFRF in general, offers us a springboard into those interesting relationships between religious belief, the government, and private institutions; in this case, whether or not the BSA—a private institution—is within its rights to exclude who it likes. We may ask, for instance, what is the difference between the BSA excluding atheists and the Masters Tournament (put on by the Professional Golf Association) excluding women? The Freedom from Religion Foundation may also prompt us to discuss and write about the plight and position of atheists in the United States, including when/how challenging religious belief is appropriate in our society?

A related question is the following: does religion, in fact, occupy a special place in our culture that makes many feel it's just best to avoid the topic altogether? In her article entitled "Dodging the God Squad," Madalyn Dawkins (a pseudonym) suggests that it does. She is a faculty member married to a senior college administrator, and says, "I've spent most of my professional life avoiding the subject of religion" (1). She cites a number of examples where college and university administrators have paid a price for either implying or explicitly stating opinions on religious belief, including "Gordon Gee's fall from the presidency of Ohio State for making derogatory statements about Roman Catholics" (2). When it comes to administrators and their spouses, the author offers a number of tips for "dodging the god squad," as she puts it, including "keep your religious (or nonreligious) beliefs to yourself" and "never make negative comments about a religion or a religious belief, even in casual conversation" (2). She concludes by writing that "in colleges nowadays, we all celebrate diversity. Unfortunately that tolerance does not extend to matters of religious belief, or lack thereof, if you are a senior administrator" (3). The fact that the author felt compelled to use a pseudonym and withhold the identity of her university provides a spark for us to discuss and write about her argument in the composition class.

In our search for material, election time is often ripe with opportunities for working with religion in the first-year writing course. During the 2012 presidential campaign, one student in my basic writing course wrote a paper arguing that Rick Perry should be the next president of the United States. It was a well written paper that earned an A, despite a weak paragraph touting his family values and moral leadership that seemed to come straight from Fox News. By chance, a few weeks after this paper was written, Perry came out with a new TV ad that captured the gist of my student's paper. After a few serious gaffes, Perry had fallen hard in the polls, and this ad was part of an attempt to regain some ground. Dressed casually and strolling outdoors, he says,

> I'm not ashamed to admit that I'm a Christian, but you don't need to be in the pew every Sunday to know that there's something wrong in this country when gays can openly serve in the military but our kids can't openly celebrate Christmas or pray in schools. As president, I'll end Obama's war on religion and I'll fight against liberal attacks on our religious heritage [Perry].

We now know the outcome of his campaign, and may feel that Perry's loss is an indicator that religious belief no longer plays such a powerful role in deciding elections. A strong case can be made, though, that the campaigns of candidates like Rick Perry and Rick Santorum were not the waning moments of an overtly religious, George W. Bush–era, socially conservative platform. With a few tweaks, their approach could very well be the future winning ticket for the Republican party. For instance, Ross Douthat writes that "Santorum's coalition is roughly the same one that Mike Huckabee tried to assemble in 2008. With a demographic mix of evangelicals and blue-collar Republicans," Douthat argues, "and a message that's conservative on social issues but more populist than the party's Wall Street wing on economics, it's proven capable of delivering states from Minnesota to Mississippi, the Rockies to the Rust Belt" (2).

Douthat recognized that like Huckabee, Santorum would probably not get the nomination. But, he said, given Santorum's "weaknesses, [both] structural and personal … it's remarkable how far he's come, and how durable this coalition has proven itself from one cycle to another." For a "candidate with more money, more policy substance, and more finesse on culture-war issues … the overall strategy might offer a blueprint for winning a future Republican primary campaign" (2).

For a lot of Americans, Douthat admits, "there's a tendency to see social conservatism as inherently backward-looking, and to assume that Santorum's campaign must be the last gasp of the Republican Party's most reactionary remnant." Underneath much of the hubris, however, lie some domestic arguments that may resonate with today's voters: "the link between family breakdown and economic disarray," for example, and the way in which we have become a country where "sky-high economic expectations coexist with middle class wage stagnation, and where the idealization of married life coexists with steadily rising out-of-wedlock births" (3).

Douthat concludes by suggesting that if—and it is a big "if"—Republican presidential candidates in the future can improve upon the "Huckabee-Santorum template," it is "possible that what Santorum has accomplished in the last few months will be remembered, not as the last glimpse of the Republican past, but as a plausible sketch of the Republican future" (3).

Others have made a similar observation. A well-financed campaign, grounded in faith with an eye to economic concerns and family structure could very well win the White House. And that is worth writing about in the socially and politically astute composition class.

In addition to election time, we can, of course, also look back to the early years of our republic when working with religious belief. To say the least, much has been written about religion during this time period, especially about the roles that deism and Christianity played as our founding fathers formed the new country. Here I mention a few brief examples of people and movements from these early years (up through the civil war) that may prove useful for us to focus upon regarding religion as a public presence and, more specifically, regarding the role it played in developing our colleges and universities.

Samuel Williams, a pastor in the First Church of Bradford, Massachusetts, saw religious belief as both public and private. In a 1779 sermon, as Frank Lambert notes, Williams argued that "religion is a *private thing*," that it is a "personal transaction between God and a devout soul" (1). But in the same sermon, he says too that "religion is also a *public* concern" and that Christianity is "well adapted to do the most essential service to Civil society" through the teaching of its values (2). This latter perspective, as Lambert shows, was indeed a popular one, one that could also been seen in the preaching of Ezra Stiles Ely in the early 1800s. Ely argued, "We are a Christian nation: we have a right to demand that all our rulers in their conduct shall conform to Christian morality; and if they do not, it is the duty and privilege of Christian freemen to make a new and a better election" (2–3). This was the sentiment, more or less, that sent Roger Williams to found Rhode Island.

There were, of course, other perspectives, including the one spawned by the Great Awakening and New Birth movements of the mideighteenth century. One could argue that the pragmatism of Peirce, James, and Dewey—with its focus on experience and change—found some roots here, where "personal experience, not belief in a church creed, not acceptance of doctrine, not submission to church authority, not the teachings of learned ministers," was central (Lambert 21). And, like Peirce, James and Dewey, these movements were leery of logically spun ontological claims: "To them, seminaries were mere factories spewing out theologians, many of whom had never experienced the New Birth, who crafted doctrines that they then imposed on parishioners. Suspicious of what they called religion of the 'head,' they favored religion of the 'heart,' the powerful emotional experience" which led to meaning and light (21). These approaches to religious belief worked as well to help define the United States of America.

An often overlooked voice with respect to religion during the nineteenth century comes from Robert Ingersoll. A friend of Henry Ward Beecher's, Ingersoll was an agnostic—referred to at times as the Great Agnostic—who worked to shepherd the country as it grappled to form a secular/religious identity. A powerful and popular speaker, Ingersoll's "appeal as a freethinker cut across political and class boundaries," and, as reported about one particular lecture in Iowa, "most of those attending ... were orthodox religious believers who nevertheless appreciated Ingersoll's wit at the expense of their own faith" (Jacoby 24). Rather than hit people over the head with aggressive certainty, Ingersoll took a lighter and more playful approach. He did not, as Susan Jacoby puts it, tell audiences "that they were simply *wrong* about what they had been taught since birth. Everyone who paid to hear Ingersoll speak knew that he or she would go away with the memory of good laughs to accompany unsettling new thoughts" (26). Nor was he a social Darwinist. Much as Charles Peirce would say, Ingersoll did not believe society should be ruled by a "survival of the fittest" look-out-for-yourself attitude, but rather a civic evolutionary approach that included love and empathy.

We could use more voices like Ingersoll's today. Most were inclined to listen to him as he was engaging instead of antagonistic. Today, when we think of the Left and the Right in the United States, it's hard to imagine a figure who can truly appeal to both.

In looking back at our country's history and growth in order to write about religion, it's worth considering, in particular, the roots and development of U.S. colleges and universities. Today most colleges and universities are seen as bastions of liberal or progressive thinking, and therefore enemies of religion. Early in our Republic, however, this was not the case. For instance, Andrew Delbanco writes, "In short, the American college was conceived from the start ... as the historian Samuel Eliot Morison put it, 'to develop the whole man—his body and soul as well as his intellect' toward the formation of a person inclined to 'unity, gentility, and public service'" (40). Ralph Waldo Emerson, in fact, put it in decidedly non-secular terms: deep down, students desire "awakening," and the teacher's job is to get the "soul out of bed" (45).

While outlining the origins of colleges and universities in the United States, Delbanco also points to William Perry, an educational psychologist writing a few decades after Emerson. Perry argued that truly effective education requires a college student to

> Accommodate uncertainty, paradox, and the demands of greater complexity. [Such a process] begins with simplistic forms in which a person construes his world in unqualified polar terms of absolute right-

wrong, good-bad; it ends with those complex forms through which he undertakes to affirm his own commitments in a world of contingent knowledge and relative values [46].

Such a process had, and still has, everything to do with aligning theistic and secular beliefs for the good of us all.

With respect to this kind of alignment in the college classroom, Delbanco touches on something I talk about at different points in this book, and that is those mysterious in-between spaces where faith and reason may roll up and play together. "Every true teacher," he writes, "understands that, along with teacher and students, a mysterious third force is present in every classroom. Sometimes this force works in favor of learning; sometimes it works against it." He adds that "the Puritan word for this invisible and inaudible force was grace. One does not need to share their belief—or to be a believer in any conventional sense—to understand what they meant" (48). One example of this space that Delbanco offers is a poem by Emily Dickenson that he and his students were working with. After different interpretations, including one student relating the poem to her own marriage, Delbanco writes that "what we concluded at the end of our discussion was not that one side or the other had won the day on behalf of its preferred reading, but that the poem existed in the difference between them" (59).

In some ways, talk of a space like this reminds me of a discussion I had once with my students about luck and momentum. Trying to make a connection to religion, I'd asked them to consider what belief in either momentum or luck might do for us, instead of arguing over whether or not they actually exist. In a sporting event, for instance, are there tangible consequences for a team and its fans who feel momentum has swung its way? Are there consequences for the other team and its fans? Likewise, what are the consequences for a gambler, or any person, who feels she is down on her luck? Much as Delbanco says about the Dickenson poem, we sort of said that luck and momentum, based on the effects they have upon us, exist only in the ever-changing space (or difference) between people and events. We know these concepts from how we behave.

One student involved in this conversation (I'll call him Jeff) ended up writing about religious belief. He'd identified himself in no uncertain terms as a far-left, secular democrat. Jerry Falwell had just died, and we talked about his influence and the legacy he left behind, including Liberty

University which he founded in 1971. Jeff ended up focusing on Falwell and Pat Robertson; he argued, more or less, that religion had run its course and was no longer needed in today's public/political world. He found some material on Falwell, most of which condemned the man as a dangerous crank. Jeff noted, for instance, that Senator John McCain, during his campaign in 2000, called Jerry Falwell and Pat Robertson "agents of intolerance," but in May 2006 McCain was the commencement speaker at Falwell's Liberty University—a university that then boasted the best college debate team in the country, for as Falwell urged, "our football program can't change the culture ... our debate team can ... our goal is to create an army of people who know how to make our case" (Chafets 52). In the past, my student observed, Falwell had argued that Jews cannot go to heaven, that we should "blow [the terrorists] all away in the name of the Lord," and that "the pagans, the abortionists, and the feminists, and the gays and the lesbians ... the A.C.L.U. ... all of them who have tried to secularize America—I point the finger in their face and say, 'you helped [Sept. 11] happen'" (Krugman A21). Regarding education, Falwell also said, "I hope to see the day when ... we won't have any public schools. The churches will have taken them over again and Christians will be running them. What a happy day that will be" (ReligiousTolerance.org 2).

Jeff linked these opinions to McCain and to politics in general. He pointed to a source that says McCain "obviously believes that he can't get the Republican nomination without Mr. Falwell's approval," and he pointed to McCain himself who said, "I believe that the Christian right has a major role to play in the Republican Party. One reason is because they're so active and their followers are" (Krugman A21). Jeff was also making the general claim that Falwell had been instrumental in the Republican Party's success since the Nixon administration. Much of what he said could be supported by evidence, but the drift of where he was going seemed to be not much more than Falwell's beliefs were wrong and that Jeff couldn't stand the guy (even though he had never met him).

I suggested that he needed to consider what tangible harm had been done to our society, trying to steer him back to the verb "does" (Falwell's beliefs did such and such) and away from the verb "is" (Falwell's beliefs were bad). In particular, I remember too bringing up the Jesuit university system that spans the globe, and I said he should do some research on what they and other universities rooted in religion have done in the world. We also talked a bit about the history of our college and university system that I mentioned above—I asked him to look into that history and then ask himself how Falwell's university is out of line with it. Or how it's different from Georgetown, a prominent university in that Jesuit web. If these universities are in fact out of sync with what we have been doing or what we should be doing in higher education in this country, why? Be specific. And focus on what they do, not on whether their beliefs are essentially right, or stupid, or crazy.

Much has been said about the relationship between the so-called religious right (including Jerry Falwell) and the Republican party over the last several decades, especially the first decade of the new millennium: see, for instance, *With God on Their Side: How Christian Fundamentalists Trampled Science, Policy, and Democracy in George W. Bush's White House* by Esther Kaplan; *American Theocracy: The Peril and Politics of Radical Religion, Oil, and Borrowed Money in the 21st Century* by Kevin Phillips; and *The Family: The Secret Fundamentalism at the Heart of American Power* by Jeff Sharlet. There is, to be sure, a lot to work with here from all three branches of our government, and over the years I've had a number of students grapple with this affiliation. Often, though, "grappling" ends up being little more than pushing an already established agenda, like my student Jeff did with Falwell. What follows are other examples worth our attention but that often get oversimplified or are trotted out to support infallible ideology.

One popular figure from the judiciary is U.S. Supreme Court Justice Antonin Scalia. Appointed by Ronald Reagan in 1986, Scalia has been vocal about the role religion plays when writing his decisions, and he attracts attention because of his hand in cases like *Bush v. Gore* in 2000. He is a devout Catholic, and the extent to which he believes his faith should propel public policy can be gleaned rather easily from passages like this one:

> The reaction of people of faith to this tendency of democracy to
> obscure the divine authority behind government should not be resig-
> nation to it, but the resolution to combat it as effectively as possible.
> We have done that in this country (and continental Europe has not) by
> preserving in our public life many visible reminders that—in the

words of a Supreme Court opinion from the 1940s—"we are a religious people, whose institutions presuppose a Supreme Being...." All this, as I say, is most unEuropean, and helps explain why our people are more inclined to understand, as Saint Paul did, that government carries the sword as "the minister of God" to "execute wrath" upon the evildoer [19].

Scalia's record as a Supreme Court Justice aligns well with how he articulates his deeply held religious beliefs. In the same speech, for example, we can see a bit of what underlies his position on the death penalty:

This is not the Old Testament, I emphasize, but St. Paul.... [T]he *core* of his message is that government—however you want to limit that concept—derives its moral authority from God.... Indeed, it seems to me that the more Christian a country is the *less* likely it is to regard the death penalty as immoral.... I attribute that to the fact that, for the believing Christian, death is no big deal. Intentionally killing an innocent person is a big deal: it is a grave sin, which causes one to lose his soul. But losing this life, in exchange for the next?... For the nonbeliever, on the other hand, to deprive a man of his life is to end his existence. What a horrible act! [18].

With respect to religion and the executive branch, references to comments by George W. Bush are legion: "I've heard the call—I believe God wants me to run for President" (Kaplan 3). Or when Bob Woodward asked him if he had consulted his father before invading Iraq, Bush responded, "You know, he is the wrong father to appeal to in terms of strength ... there is a higher father that I appeal to" (Woodward 421). When writing about the way in which religious belief informed the presidency of George W. Bush, one of my students referred to the following. In a meeting with Israel's Ariel Sharon and Palestine's new Prime Minister Mahmoud Abbas, it's reported that Bush said, "God told me to strike at al–Qaeda and I struck them, and then he instructed me to strike at Saddam Hussein, which I did" (Kamen). Other references to Bush's religion include comments by people like Jeffrey S. Siker, a highly regarded Catholic theologian, who has noted that in general "we have had other 'religious' presidents ... but no other president has so clearly perceived his calling in such epic biblical terms." In the same article, Siker goes on to add that Bush saw "America as a kind of new Israel called by God to be God's people on the international stage," and that through his born-again experience he now had "a clear vision of what is morally right and wrong," a vision which holds that "some people simply deserve the wrathful judgment of God, and if God chooses to use him as the vehicle of punishment, so be it ... whether for death row inmates in Texas or for governments such as Iraq" (1). Bush has been an easy target for atheists, but we're often left to wonder what exactly is being criticized—the practical consequences of his belief, or just his belief.

I have had students write about the way in which religious belief influences legislators as well: references to Tom Delay stick most in my mind. Usually the papers I've received offer little that is new or nuanced, and I've found myself reminding them that whether we're working with judges, presidents, lawmakers, or anyone else, our focus must be on the societal consequences of a particular belief—or, to steal from Updike, it must be on the right "end of the stick." Moreover, as most of us teach in composition classes anyway, it's usually a good thing to consider those on the other side of the field. In this particular case, it's certainly not just the Republicans in our government who reference or rely upon religious belief. As Howard Dean was about to become chairman of the Democratic party, he said, "Democrats had the real claim on religious values because of their commitment to help the poor and the afflicted." The same article quotes Dr. Dean as saying, "when you think of the New Testament, [the Republicans] get about 2 of the values and we get about 27" (Kornblut). Positioning herself for the Democratic nomination in 2008, Hillary Clinton started to tap into America's religious vein as well. In response to a border protection and illegal immigration bill proposed by Bill Frist in the Senate, Clinton stated that it was "certainly not in keeping with my understanding of the Scripture because this bill would literally criminalize the Good Samaritan and probably even Jesus himself" (Bernstein).

This particular bill actually attracted a lot of attention, especially from the United States Conference of Catholic Bishops. In particular, Roger Mahony, the cardinal archbishop of Los Angeles, instructed his parishioners to oppose the bill because, in part, it would "subject to five years in prison anyone who 'assists' an undocumented immigrant to 'remain in the United States'" (Mahony A29). Like many others, Cardinal Mahony is still pushing for more comprehensive immigration reform, arguing that "providing humanitarian assistance to those in need should not be made a crime" and reminding us that "current law does not require social service agencies to obtain evidence of legal status before rendering aid, nor should it. Denying aid to a fellow human being violates a law with a higher authority than Congress—the law of God" (A29). In this particular article, Mahony makes some compelling arguments to further his cause, and concludes by saying "the church is compelled to take a stand against harmful legislation and to work towards positive change" (A29). Mahony, in fact, has become quite a controversial figure, less for his stance on immigration and more for his role in the sexual abuse crisis his church has had to face. He is an interesting person for us to focus on in the composition class.

With respect to addressing the flip side of an argument, for those bent on how Republicans use religion we can point to other Democrats, of course, besides Howard Dean and Hillary Clinton. Barack Obama is an obvious example. In chapter 1, I brought up a speech that Obama gave on religion in 2006; we can also look to his remarks at the 2013 National Prayer Breakfast. He calls us to take "real and meaningful action" and to do so with "open hearts and open minds," and the call is, of course, given the setting, a deeply religious one. He quotes a passage from the Book of Hebrews: "Without faith it is impossible to please God, because anyone who comes to Him must believe that He exists and He rewards those who diligently seek Him." Obama adds that "He rewards those who diligently seek Him—not just for one moment, or one day, but for every moment, and every day" ("Remarks" 3). He then states the following: "As Christians, we place our faith in the nail-scarred hands of Jesus Christ. But so many other Americans also know the close embrace of faith—Muslims and Jews, Hindus and Sikhs. And all Americans—whether religious or secular—have a deep and abiding faith in this nation" (3). He refers to the Bibles that were owned by Abraham Lincoln and Martin Luther King and how those men were inspired and fortified by their religion, and he ends by asking us to "pray to God that we may be worthy of the many blessings He has bestowed upon our nation" (7). We might ask, in the writing class, how are these comments different from those that George W. Bush so often made with respect to religion? What do they do for us that is better or different from religious speeches by Bush, or Rick Santorum, or Rick Perry?

The Weight of Authority

Even if we are talking about public as opposed to private religious belief in the composition class, there is probably an elephant in the room that still needs to be addressed. It would be reasonable to ask, despite a middle-ground approach based on careful, pragmatic formulations, how a writing teacher competes with a lifetime of instruction by parents and clergy? The answer, I believe, is that teachers shouldn't see themselves as having to compete. In a more academic sense, we don't have to compete because, as Santiago Zabala suggests, "after modernity, there are no more strong philosophical reasons either to be an atheist refusing religion or to be a theist refusing science; the deconstruction of metaphysics has cleared the ground for a culture without those dualisms.... In this postmodern condition, faith ... absorbs these dualisms without recognizing in them any reasons for conflict" (Rorty and Vattimo 2). In a less academic sense, we don't have to compete simply because our particular approach says so. Our parameters do not include which side can prove an ultimate Truth. We proceed in terms of interrogating our various habits with respect to a volatile social issue for the purpose of further reflection. In addition, we shouldn't feel the need to compete with religious dogma when we prompt our students to ask hard questions because questioning authority has never been an exclusively secular practice. Various branches of Christianity, for example, have always had a strong history of "bucking the system." Besides the books that I've read, I've seen evidence of this in my own family.

Although my parents and my brother and sister and I left the church when I was a teenager, we come from a strong Catholic background—most of my extended family (and being Catholic, there are lots of us) still attend church on a regular basis and to varying degrees are motivated by their religion. When my paternal grandmother died, my aunt Jeannie read a moving piece at the funeral. At one point, she described how my grandma withdrew her membership from "Daughters of the Revolution" because this storied organization began to align itself with racist policies. My aunt relayed how sad and angry my grandma was about the whole episode—for years she was proud of her membership in this group, but she couldn't condone or be associated with what it had become. In many ways her membership in this group had been intimately bound up with her faith and her church, but Jeannie quoted my grandma as saying, "being Catholic means helping people, and to help people we have to try to make things better. A lot of times that means changing what you've been doing, even if you've been doing it for a long time and you don't really want to [change]." Most of the Catholics I know, both family members and other acquaintances, have given me the impression that their faith is not synonymous with blind obedience. I've heard them disagree with their pastors, argue over the meaning of scripture, etc. In other words, for these people who I know, the word of God is subject to change and interpretation.

As I was beginning to think about this project, I came across an article in *Time* magazine that seemed to sum up for me much of the attitude that my relatives take towards religious belief. Regarding the current sexual abuse crisis in the Catholic Church, this issue advertises on the cover "Catholics in Revolt" in reference to its article, "Rebels in the Pews: No Matter What Their Bishops Decide, Catholic Lay People Say It Is Time for Their Voice to Be Heard." The article recounts how practitioners have formed groups across the country and called for reform, like the "'Voice of the Faithful,' which wants to turn the church into a representative democracy" (Biema 55). The article ends with a confessional titled, "Who Says the Church Can't Change?: An Anguished Catholic Argues That Loving the Church Means Reforming It" (63). Here, Andrew Sullivan articulates some of what I hear from my relatives and also some of what I hear in the pragmatism I describe in chapter 2. "Even when [the Church] inflicted real pain," Sullivan says, "when it callously treated women as second-class Catholics, when it wounded good people in bad marriages, when it penetrated into the souls of young gay kids and made them hate themselves, I knew that it was a human institution on a divine mission. Human institutions fail. But, I reminded myself, they can also change" (63). While John Dewey may question the reference to a "divine mission," he, as well as Peirce, James, and the Catholics in my family, would likely champion the notion that change does not mean discarding one's faith. On the contrary. As Sullivan concludes with respect to the sexual abuse scandals, "what we have witnessed means we would be delinquent if we didn't fight for real change. We are actually being more faithful than those who want to perpetuate the conditions for further decline" (64).

While many scholars and theists would support Sullivan's position, there persists the popular notion that iron-clad dogma dictates the behavior of all worshipers. For instance, as Mano Singham describes in his book *Quest for Truth*, a common perception of "religious belief structures [is that they] usually have an unchanging core" and that followers "do not probe for inconsistencies or periodically replace their old beliefs with new ones in the light of new knowledge. Indeed, the unchanging nature of core religious beliefs is considered to be one of its main virtues, a reflection of its eternal truth" (167). There are, to be sure, worshipers who understand their faith in these terms. What Singham describes, however, is only one perspective. In "The Dogma of Inquiry: Composition and the Primacy of Faith," for example, Jeffrey M. Ringer writes that "there's a difference between dogma that precludes inquiry and dogma that serves as the starting place for asking questions" (350). In describing the difference between dogmatic discourse of affirmation and dogmatic discourse of inquiry, Ringer points to St. Augustine and Lesslie Newbigin as illustrations of the latter, illustrations of what Ringer calls "humble dogma," a dogma that prompts the kind of reflection and critical thinking that writing teachers generally encourage.

For other examples of such "humble dogma," we may look as well to various interpretations of the Bible. As Alicia Ostriker notes, for example, a close reading of "the Bible is to recognize that sacred writ is intrinsically no more absolute in its authority than any other writing" (61). Ostriker adds that

> the questioning of authority, including divine authority, has been built into Judaism in several different ways. From the moment God confides to Abraham his intention to destroy Sodom and Gomorrah, and Abraham is appalled and replies, "Shall the Judge of all the earth not do justly?"—making clear that he, Abraham, thinks God has no right to harm innocent people—the right and even the duty of God's children to interrogate their father becomes a recurrent Biblical theme [58].

In addition to the Bible, we might consider contemporary leaders of the Roman Catholic Church regarding the grip of inflexible dogma. With respect to the Church's position on gender roles, Carol Jablonski writes that Pope John XXIII "helped to open up the Church's thinking on women by acknowledging, without disparagement, that women's roles are changing and by affirming that women can contribute to society by working outside the home" (165). In the mid–1960s, in fact, the pope put forth an aggressive human rights agenda, asserting that "every type of discrimination, whether social or cultural, whether based on sex, race, color, social condition, language, or religion, is to be overcome and erad-icated as contrary to God's intent" (166). In our effort to bridge the gap between the goals of a critical liberatory writing course and students who may hold fundamentalist beliefs, we can look to the work of this pope which in large part posits that reinterpretation and critical thinking are not only possible but necessary aspects of a healthy religious faith. In framing a discussion about the institution of marriage, for instance, we might point to his statement that "human beings have the right to choose freely the state of life which they prefer" (166).

I mention two other popes here briefly to help develop this example. There appears to be new evidence (or at least a new focus on old evi-dence) with respect to the role that Pope Pius XII played during World War II. During the war itself, the pope was seen as a savior to Jews and others victimized by the Nazis. But press from the Soviet Union together with other forces, such as questions like why he never spoke out against Hitler, worked to paint a dark picture of the Vatican during this period. It now seems, though, that the pope had his reasons for staying silent, and, as we see in a new book by Gordon Thomas entitled *The Pope's Jews: The Vatican's Secret Plan to Save Jews from the Nazis*, those reasons worked to save a lot of people. Pius XII put in place a web of secret loca-tions to hide those running from the Nazis, especially in Rome after Mussolini fell in 1943. Upon closer inspection, it appears the actions of this pope did quite a bit of good.

My final example from the Vatican is more recent: Pope Benedict XVI. His was not exactly a liberal papacy. He did little to improve the sexual abuse crisis in the Church, nor did he take a liberal approach to issues like homosexuality and the ordination of women. The way he left, however, was striking. He gave us, in the words of Jon Meacham, "some-thing rare among the most mighty: an example of Christian piety that was quite unexpected" (24). In the face of tradition (no pope has resigned in the last six centuries), he looked to lived experience and he acted. Having watched his predecessor slowly decline and suffer during the last years of his life, Benedict XVI came to believe that a pope could retire if "he is no longer physically, psychologically and spiritually capable of handling the duties of his office" (Chua-Eoan 20). Under these circumstances, he felt that any pope had the "right and, under some circumstances, also an obligation to resign" (20). His final act as pope was, in short, quite pragmatic, and it will be interesting to see what happens with his successor.

Popes, of course, are only one example when it comes to authority and orthodoxy. There are countless "high-profile" and "low-profile" people of faith who we can enlist to help us question what has been handed to us. Mary Daly, for instance, who, as a Catholic, worked to make God a "verb who is the most active of all verbs" and strove to reclaim for women "the power of their own speech" within the Catholic Church (Jablonski 168). Or Jeffrey Cain, who, in "(Sacra) Mentality: Catholic Identity in the Postmodern Classroom," concludes that "the organism of religion absolutely requires doubt, without which there would be no fall from grace, no test of faith, no teleology. Doubt thus plays a positive role, since uncertainty provides a moment of flight from absolute authority, and it is in this moment that immanence unfolds itself" (179). Likewise, in a book review of Nel Noddings' *Educating for Intelligent Belief and Unbelief*, Todd DeStigter writes that while "Noddings doesn't say so explicitly, at the core of her ambitious project is the need to foster in teachers an understanding of faith that I once heard articulated from a Presbyterian pulpit: 'The opposite of faith is not doubt; the opposite of faith is certainty'" (78). In short, what I've learned from my reading is often consistent with the "critical faith" I have seen and heard from many members of my own family. In their homes, at church, and on the street, it seems safe to conclude that vast numbers of worshipers see religion as intricately bound up with critical inquiry—which is good for us in the composition class, as critical inquiry is something we tend to like.

We can, specifically, connect the "re-visioning" of religious doctrine discussed above with how most writing teachers already talk about revising and the day-to-day happy grind of composing. We need to constantly revisit what we write to try to make it better (to steal from Paul Valery, writing is never finished, it's only turned in). We have to question what we write. Revise what we write. Ask ourselves how this part or that part fits with the rest of what we are trying to say. How does this particular paragraph support the main idea? Is this paragraph even necessary? Just because we wrote it doesn't mean we *have* to keep it. If it's not useful, cut it. And we do this together, with input from as many people as possible. All of this—based on experience, context, cohesion, collaboration—directs our writing process *and* our way in to what we are writing about. Revision (too often met with dread) should be presented as part of the fun. As Susan Sontag says, getting started is hard; sitting down to write can be "formidable, intimidating. A plunge in an icy lake." But rewriting (together with rereading) is, as she says, "the most pleasurable part ... the warm part, when you already have something to work with, upgrade, edit" (264). Re-vision is not just vital for writing, religion, and for writing about religion. It's "the most pleasurable part."

Habit and Attitude

Whether it comes to questioning authority or clipping our fingernails, we do almost everything out of habit. We are, as they say, that kind of creature. In his book *Talks to Teachers*, William James, in fact, tells us that "Ninety-nine hundredths ... of our activity is purely automatic and habitual, from our rising in the morning to our lying down each night" (57). I think he's right, at least when it comes to mayonnaise. I'd been mixing tuna fish with Miracle Whip since I was old enough to make it myself, and before that it's how my mom used to make it as well. I would spread more mayo on the bread, and then add three or four nice chunks of cheddar cheese. "Next time I'll make it for you," Sonia said when she first saw this. "With regular yogurt, *sin sabor*, and a little mustard." "Mustard?" I said. "You don't mix mustard with tuna fish."

But that's how I ate it the next time, and that is how I'm in the habit of eating it now (no more cheddar, either). We are creatures of habit, James said, mainly because we have bodies. "The plasticity of the living matter of our nervous system," he writes,

> is the reason why we do a thing with difficulty the first time, but soon do it more and more easily, and finally, with sufficient practice, do it semi-mechanically, or with hardly any consciousness at all. Our nervous systems have (in Dr. Carpenter's words) *grown* to the way in which they have been exercised, just as a sheet of paper or a coat, once creased or folded, tends to fall forever afterward into the same identical fold [57].

Adding a new crease to that sheet of paper is difficult, but can be done. When attempting to change any habitual behavior—the food we eat, the language we speak, the way we see science and religious belief—we have to work to "make our nervous systems our ally instead of our enemy" (93). I remember preparing for an uphill battle as I tried to learn a second language at the age of thirty-five. Like a lot of people, I thought it was much easier to learn one as a child, or early teenager, before the mind began to congeal and "set" in its ways. As it turns out, though, this may not really be true.

Decades of research have suggested that adults don't necessarily lose their ability to learn another language as they get older (see, for example, Krashen, Long, and Scarcella; see also Otswald and Williams). In fact, if we stay healthy, we actually gain a few things that children and teens don't have, such as enhanced critical thinking skills, more motivation, and a bank of experience from which to draw upon. Contrary to earlier theories from the '50s and '60s that suggested the brain begins to lose "cerebral plasticity" once we hit puberty, most experts now say that on average "adults have superior language learning capabilities" (Walsh and Diller 12).

One well known theory of language acquisition is Stephen Krashen's monitor hypothesis. As our native tongue is acquired, not learned, we are able to speak it without first checking or scanning what we say to see if we are saying it correctly. While we're learning a second language, though, Krashen suggests that we consciously monitor what we are saying before we try to say it. One part of this hypothesis is what he calls the Affective Filter, which can work to impede an adult's ability to learn another language. Simply put, this filter is connected to the learner's mood and emotions: if she is angry, anxious, or otherwise agitated, the filter is thick and learning is blocked. If she is relaxed, with a positive attitude towards the second language and those who speak it, the filter is thin and learning passes more freely (see Krashen, *Principles*). This filter is generally not found in children as they have less conscious control over their emotions and fewer pre-existing assumptions from which to raise walls of objections (Gass 402). Adults, however, both have the filter and, if they choose, are able to control it.

Krashen's argument makes sense to me when I think of my own experience learning Spanish. How well I speak it still depends on when, where, and with whom I'm speaking. Sometimes I amaze myself: I'll rattle off a sentence I had no idea I knew how to say, or I'll screw up a simple phrase that I'd learned a long time ago. For example, after teaching all month in Santiago for not many pesos (or, as they say, for my "bolsitas de dulces"), I understood almost nothing and could say almost nothing to the people who kept telling me my check was on the way. Usually the delay was my fault—I'd forgotten to do something or sign something. But that didn't matter much. I was frustrated, and in that moment I had little or no interest in the language or those who were using it.

Krashen's argument also makes sense to me when I think of theists and atheists as speaking different languages. If an effort was made by all involved to "thin" our filters—or to work on adding a new crease to that "sheet of paper" William James talked about—communication and learning might flow more easily when it comes to thinking and writing about Darwin and Jesus.

CHAPTER 4

God in the Comp Class: Assignments (and Responding to Assignments)

> [Writing] is about developing a rational
> grace and energy in your conversation
> with the world around you.
> —Verlyn Klinkenborg

> We are saved not by a special apparatus
> known as religion, but by the quality of
> our everyday relations with one another.
> —Terry Eagleton

> If we are to avail ourselves of that
> incomparable resource, the minds of our
> students, we will have to know what we're
> looking for, to have some philosophically
> sound idea of the power the mind promises.
> I believe that for teachers of composition,
> such a philosophy of mind is best thought
> of as a theory of imagination.
> —Ann Berthoff

For our purposes, we can think of Ann Berthoff's "theory of imagination" in the sense that we're asking students to imagine, or reimagine, religious belief in a particular kind of way, a way that has to do with how we interact and converse with the world around us. Framing the issue like this opens up a greater number of possibilities for writing and talking about religion, as we don't begin with foregone conclusions (God is great, God is not great) but begin with the countless possibilities prompted by asking what religion does in the world. It's here where things can open up, where, as Berthoff says, the power of chaos can be put to use, as chaos provides choices, and choices can fuel imagination. The parameters set by our pragmatic approach help students to see religion in a different light and offer more choices when considering this topic; students are in a better position, then, to take advantage of that initial chaotic, ambiguous moment that Berthoff says is so important when it comes to writing. But our "students cannot learn the uses of chaos," she adds, "if we continue to make assignments appropriate not to these beginnings but to the final [rigid] phases of the composing process" (70).

In chapter 3, I discussed a couple of essays and explored several places to look in setting some borders for working with religion in the writing class. In this chapter, I highlight other texts teachers might include on the syllabus, some that will look familiar and others that might not. I then turn to ten student essays on religion written in response to three different writing assignments. My hope in this chapter is to shed more light on ways in which students may be prompted to imagine and reimagine religious belief as they converse with the world around them.

Chekov's "The Student" and Porter's "Granny Weatherall"

I came across the first text I want to suggest while at a talk by Cornel West when I was in graduate school. At one point, while answering a question about his religion and the way in which it informed his thinking and his writing, he brought up Chekhov's "The Student." "There are some answers in there," he said. So that weekend, I read it.

He was right, and I've since taught this story a number of times. It's about a young clerical student who is walking home on a cold and desolate evening, an evening that was for the most part "cheerless, remote, and lonely" (106). It was also Good Friday. Bracing against the chill and thinking of the profound religious implications of the day, the student imagined

> that just such a wind had blown in the days of Rurik and in the time of Ivan the Terrible and Peter, and in their time there had been just

the same desperate poverty and hunger, the same thatched roofs with holes in them, ignorance, misery, the same desolation around, the same darkness, the same feeling of oppression—all these had existed, did exist, and would exist, and the lapse of a thousand years would make life no better. And he did not want to go home [106].

He stops at a fire attended by a mother and daughter (the daughter, Chekhov tells us, "had often been beaten by her husband"), and after their greetings, the student says, "At just such a fire the Apostle Peter warmed himself ... so it must have been cold then too. Ah, what a terrible night it must have been, granny! An utterly dismal long night!" (107). He then tells the story of Peter at the Last Supper, and how he told Jesus that he would go with Him into darkness and death. But Jesus responds, "I say unto thee, Peter, before the cock croweth, thou wilt have denied Me thrice" (107). This comes to pass, of course—before dawn, Peter denies that he knows or has spent time with Him on three different occasions. The student goes on, telling his listeners by the fire that when the cock crowed, Peter remembered what Jesus had said, and he "went out of the yard and wept bitterly—bitterly.... I imagine it: the still, still, dark, dark garden, and in the stillness, faintly audible, smothered sobbing" (108).

"Still smiling," Chekhov writes, the mother "gave a gulp, big tears flowed freely down her face, and she screened her face from the fire" (108). The daughter, with a dumbfounded look on her face, "flushed crimson, and her expression became strained and heavy like that of someone enduring intense pain" (108). The student heads home and thinks about the women's reaction to his story, and decides that "it was evident that what he had just been telling them about, which had happened nineteen centuries ago, had a relation to the present—to both women, to the desolate village, to himself, to all people. The old woman had wept, not because he could tell the story touchingly, but because Peter was near to her, because her whole being was interested in what was passing in Peter's soul" (108). As the student reflects on this, "joy suddenly stirred in his soul, and he even stopped for a minute to take a breath. 'The past,' he thought, 'is linked with the present by an unbroken chain of events flowing one out of another.' And it seemed to him that he had just seen both ends of that chain; that when he touched one end the other quivered" (108).

105

Chekhov's striking metaphor of an unbroken chain that links us to one another across time may certainly be read as something both beautiful and reassuring that religious belief can do: in addition to the old woman's revelation, the tale ends with the young student feeling healthy and strong, as "the inexpressible sweet expectations of … unknown mysterious happiness took possession of him little by little, and life seemed to him enchanting, marvelous and full of lofty meaning" (109). He has experienced a spiritual awakening similar to the religious epiphanies that Flannery O'Connor gives to so many characters in her stories or that Tolstoy's Ivan Ilych experiences towards the end of his novella, *The Death of Ivan Ilych*. In each of these cases the protagonist breaks through an unhappy mist of ennui or even a prolonged final illness to discover to his or her personal ratification that he or she is, in fact, on the "right" path. It is usually, but not always, a final, joyous moment of affirmation and encouragement. However, of course, sometimes this spiritual revelation can be sadly defeating, as in the case of Katherine Anne Porter's "The Jilting of Granny Weatherall."

In Porter's story, one that works as a powerful counterpoint to "The Student," an elderly woman is on her deathbed and is slipping in and out of consciousness. She has been a devout Christian, convinced that she will finally receive her reward of being greeted by Jesus after a faithful life in His service and in the service of her family. Her only profound struggle with what she saw as evil has been to forgive the man who long ago had left her standing at the altar, broken-hearted and devastated. That struggle to forgive was arduous, but she believes she has accomplished it. Soon after she was "jilted" by that absent bridegroom, she married a "better man," a man with whom she raised a family and built a good life according to all the rules of her church. Now, with death at hand and a candle at her bedside, she watches intently for Jesus, the final bridegroom she has been promised. But he, too, does not appear. This time the jilting is intolerable; this time she cannot forgive. And so she "blew out the light" and died (184).

Just as Chekhov's story reaffirms religious belief and demonstrates what religion can do to help humanity through its times of desolation, Porter's story provides a clear denial of faith and seems to assert the emptiness and finality of our desolation. But both stories leave room for opposing points of view. Throughout his story, Chekhov offers to non-believers a number of words that transcend dogma and invite alternate interpretations—words like "inexpressible," "unknown," "mysterious," and "enchanting" all transcend narrow explanation. Ultimately, the story's power comes not just from the Christian tradition it draws upon, but from its extraordinary ability to affect readers of all stripes with a mystifying moment of human connection. Porter leaves even more opportunities for contradiction available to her reader: throughout the story, she accumulates evidence that Ms. Weatherall has indeed "weathered all." She and her husband accomplished a great deal together, her family loves her, and there is no doubt that her faith, true or false, sustained her until the last. Its truth or falsity is not the issue, but rather what it did for her. Some of my students, in fact, have found that in her final refusal to forgive she affirms the usefulness of the Christian teaching that we must forgive. In other words, the very defiance of the rule affirms its benefit, and her last moments are darkened by flouting it.

In the past, I've had some success by asking my students to think and write about the following: does one have to believe in God or in a particular religion in order to fully appreciate either "The Student" or "Granny Weatherall"? Are religious beliefs necessary to understand the human bonds explored in these stories? Do the stories work only because of the specific references to Jesus, Peter, *et al.*? Such questions quickly illustrate that the focus in the course is not on the dogmatic Truth of the stories, but rather on how they might be useful to meaningful human interaction—and in both of these cases, by interaction that culminates in a single clarifying moment of transcendence or revelation.

Cornel West seemed to like "The Student" because it highlights the good that religious belief can do in the world. There are, of course, countless other stories that can highlight the bad, stories about the Crusades, the Spanish Inquisition, the witch trials, the sexual abuse crisis of the Catholic Church, and so on (a veritable catalog of such examples can be found in *Holy Horrors: An Illustrated History of Religious Murder and Madness* by James A. Haught). Texts that emphasize both the good and the bad, of course, must be included and addressed in the composition class to provide that balance William James refers to when he talks of the gauntlet that all our beliefs need to run; that system of checks and balances whereby each belief is only as good or as useful as our other beliefs, based on lived experience, will allow.

The Seagull Reader

Those who teach composition on a regular basis may be familiar with *The Seagull Reader: Essays* edited by Joseph Kelly. I choose to talk about this collection because I've had experience teaching both the first and second editions, I've heard several other writing teachers say they've used the book, and it does, I believe, include a number of commonly taught essays in the composition course. One of these essays is Martin Luther King Junior's "Letter from Birmingham Jail."

When I first began to teach this essay, I focused on King's rhetorical prowess, invoking Aristotle's rhetorical triangle and asking students to consider the way in which logos, ethos, and pathos come together to move the reader. Like many secularists, I imagine, I tended to see the doctor part more than the reverend part of King's prefix. I would mention that it was written by a preacher for a group of clergymen, and we would talk about how, in the latter part of the essay, King describes his disappointment with the white church, notes how one can only be deeply disappointed with something that one deeply loves, and offers hope that the church will rise to the challenge of reorienting itself. But that was as far as I would usually go. I didn't really want to dwell on religion.

According to Jonathan Rieder, however, I was missing (or avoiding) the main thrust of this essay. It is, indeed, a wonderful example of Aristotle's rhetorical triangle. But, as Rieder writes, the "image of liberal secular King misses the central role of prophetic Christianity" in most of King's work (Freedman 1). In an article on Rieder's new book entitled *Gospel of Freedom*, Samuel Freedman cites the Reverend James A. Forbes Jr., a prominent minister from King's era: "In [Rieder's] book, unlike many that speak primarily of a King that was a civil rights leader, he plumbs the depth of the spirituality out of which that leadership came" (1). King's work in general and "Letter from Birmingham Jail" in particular are extraordinary examples of what religious belief does in the world—an obvious statement, perhaps, but one that tends to get lost in the secular composition course. In fact, the religious aspect of the essay may be more important than its classic rhetorical moves: Rieder says, "In truth, the 'Letter' was less formal rhetoric or a philosophical treatise than a transcribed form of oral culture" (1), and Freedman writes, "The public Dr. King ... cannot be understood without understanding the preacher's talking black talk to black folk" (1). When we teach this essay in the comp class, we cannot skim over the role of religion.

The next essay I want to look at from the *Seagull Reader* is one that was added in the second edition, and that is "One Side Can Be Wrong" by Richard Dawkins and Jerry Coyne. Their main argument is that the theory of Intelligent Design (ID) doesn't belong in a science class because it is "not a scientific argument at all, but a religious one." They add that it may belong in a number of other classes, but "it no more belongs in a biology class than alchemy belongs in a chemistry class, phlogiston in a physics class or the stork theory in a sex education class. In those cases," they argue, "the demand for equal time for both theories would be ludicrous" (71). The authors go on to show that ID doesn't play by the same rules as other scientific theories, and that the mountain of evidence—always open to critique—from so many different fields has established evolution as "a fact: as much a fact as plate tectonics or the heliocentric solar system" (74).

In the writing class, this essay gives us a chance to teach deductive reasoning and the syllogism. In the book's introduction, Joseph Kelly talks about the different sorts of arguments writers make, including the difference between inductive and deductive lines of reasoning. We might first discuss these with our students and then offer Dawkins and Coyne's essay as an example of the latter. One argument put forth by proponents of ID, they write, is that there are countless things and creatures in the world which are far too complex to have simply evolved, so they must have been created. Dawkins and Coyne respond by saying, "The claim that something—say the bacterial flagellum—is too complex to have evolved by natural selection is alleged, by a lamentably common but false syllogism, to support the 'rival' intelligent design theory by default" (73). Going back to deductive reasoning and perhaps one famous example of a syllogism ("All men are mortal, Socrates is a man, therefore Socrates is mortal"), we can ask our students to come up with the false syllogism that the authors refer to and then to come up with a good syllogism that supporters of ID might be able to use. The first time I tried this, it didn't go as smoothly as I had hoped, but for the false syllogism we eventually arrived at something like this: "Complex things cannot evolve, X is a complex thing, therefore the theory of ID is correct." For a better syllogism that proponents of the ID theory might be able to use, we came up with something like this: "Complex things cannot evolve, X is a complex thing, therefore X could not have evolved." We were still left here with a questionable first premise, but at least we were moving in the right direction with respect to syllogisms; we were also moving away from whether or not the theory of ID is fundamentally correct and towards more useful, practical arguments.

One problem I've run into with this essay, though, is that despite the authors' careful positioning (they argue specifically that the theory of ID does not belong in a *science* class), there is an underlying feeling that religious belief is under attack. Part of this may have to do with one of the authors, Richard Dawkins. Dawkins is probably best known for his book *The God Delusion*, a book that has not put him in the good graces of many theists or, for that matter, some agnostics and atheists. For instance, Terry Eagleton lumps Dawkins and Christopher Hitchens together (Hitchens because of his book *God is Not Great: How Religion Poisons Everything*) and calls them "Ditchkins." When it comes to religion, Eagleton says that "Ditchkins" is "talking out of the back of his neck," pandering to what secularists want to hear and offering little that might be of use (2–3).

To help counter this reputation that may precede Richard Dawkins, we might refer our students to a letter that Dawkins wrote to his young daughter about religion titled "Good and Bad Reasons for Believing." I first came across this letter in a book by the Reverend Michael Dowd titled *Thank God for Evolution: How the Marriage of Science and Religion Will Transform Your Life and Our World*. Dowd included the letter because, as he says, "it powerfully distinguishes the relative value today of, what I like to call, private and public revelation" and because "it provides an invaluable critique of traditional, flat-earth faith, while offering sound guidance for an evidential, evolutionary faith" (349).

This letter highlights our need for evidence based on lived experience to understand the world around us and focuses on three things that often work to obscure such evidence: tradition, authority, and revelation. The problem with tradition, Dawkins says, is that people simply believe things because people before them "have believed the same thing over the centuries," but this fact alone doesn't make those things true. He offers the story of Mary ascending into heaven after her death, a story not mentioned in the Bible and only begun about 600 years after the death of Jesus. Over the years, though, it grew into tradition and, as Dawkins notes, it "finally was written down as an official Roman Catholic belief only very recently, in 1950" (352). He talks too about the dangers of authority, or relying on something just because someone powerful said it, and says that science too relies on authority, but the difference is that "people who wrote the [science] books have seen the evidence and anyone is free to look carefully at the evidence whenever they want" (353). And one problem with the notion of revelation, he says, is that it usually comes from the musings of just one person, uncorroborated by the experiences of others.

These problems with tradition, authority, and revelation, however, don't in and of themselves negate religious belief. As William James has said, any route to knowledge should not be summarily excluded; if it can pass the test of lived experience and run the gauntlet of our other beliefs (or to put it in Dawkins' terms, the test of evidence), then it should be heard. Dawkins talks too about love, noting that even this is eventually understood by tangible actions in the world. He says that love can be proven: "All through the day when you are with somebody who loves you, you see and hear lots of little tidbits of evidence, and they all add up ... there are outside things to back up the inside feeling: looks in the eye, tender notes in the voice, little favors and kindnesses; this is all real evidence" (354). And like love, science may start with an inside feeling, or a hunch, as Dawkins puts it, but that feeling must then be tested out in the world. So too with religion.

Sam Harris was added to the second edition of the *Seagull Reader* as well. In the eyes of many religious believers, together with Hitchens and Dawkins Harris completes an "axis of evil" aimed at attacking religion. I mentioned Harris' book *The End of Faith* in my first chapter; in *The Seagull Reader*, Kelly includes an excerpt from the same book titled "The Myth of 'Moderation' in Religion." Here, Harris argues that moderate religious believers do as much damage in the world as religious fanatics because moderates hold the same basic beliefs as fanatics and thus provide no real check or challenge to fanatical behavior. At its base, Harris says that "religious moderation is the product of *secular* knowledge and scriptural *ignorance*" (128). Moderates pick and choose what they like from the Bible, or what is convenient for them to enjoy living their lives. Ultimately, given religious conflicts that still rage in the world,

Harris suggests that we need to get past religious belief altogether in an age of nuclear weapons if we want to survive as a race.

It's easy to see how atheists may rally behind this essay and how religious believers may shake their heads and just turn away. If we move in the pragmatic direction I'm suggesting, however, we can have productive discussions in the classroom that lead to thoughtful essays. Addressing Harris directly, what might be the real consequences, both good and bad, in a world without religious belief? What would happen if people stopped cherry-picking what they liked from the Bible and lived their lives as fully secular citizens? On balance, does the chance of nuclear annihilation outweigh the good that religious belief does in the world? Harris writes that a major problem with moderation in religion is that "it has nothing underwriting it other than the unacknowledged neglect of the letter of the divine law" and that the "moderation we see among nonfundamentalists is not some sign that faith itself has evolved; it is, rather, the product of the many hammer blows of modernity that have exposed certain tenets of faith to doubt" (126). Perhaps he is right, but students and teachers in a composition course can respond by saying, So what? It doesn't concern us whether or not the Truth of religion has taken some hits, or that moderate religion is bad because of the dubious claims it ignores. Our questions concern the tangible consequences of moderate religious belief for those now here on the planet.

The last essay from *The Seagull Reader* I want to address is Bret Lott's "Atonement." Only a couple of pages long, it is rife with religious references, but not dogmatic. The essay applies phrases from the Christian tradition like "transgressions," "obeying your father," and "atonement after confession" to everyday struggles that most of us find. Frustrated over the ordinary chore of getting his kids out of the house and off to camp in the morning, Lott writes, "My world and its woes boiled down to *Why can't you just listen and obey me without making me yell*?" (218). There is no story here, he says, other than behaving badly in the face of life and then trying to make up for it with the "right word, the right gesture. The lunch at Wendy's, atonement after confession" (219). We don't encounter any church or clergymen, but a religious tradition is at work in this essay through language, karate camp, acts of reflection, and simply "being a father" (219). How it's at work is something we can talk and write about in the composition course.

In-Between Space, Gender and Race

In the movie *Contact*, Ellie, a scientist, and Palmer, a Christian philosopher, have the following exchange:

> ELLIE: All right, so what is more likely ... an all-powerful and mysterious God created the Universe and then decided not to give any proof of his existence, or that he simply doesn't exist at all, and that we created him so we don't have to feel so small and alone.
>
> PALMER: I don't know. I couldn't imagine living in a world where God didn't exist. I wouldn't want to.
>
> ELLIE: How do you know you're not deluding yourself? As for me, I'd need proof.
>
> PALMER: Proof [he pauses]. Did you love your father?
>
> ELLIE: Huh?
>
> PALMER: Your dad, did you love him?
>
> ELLIE: Yes, very much.
>
> PALMER: Prove it.

Ellie does not know how to prove it, and the scene leaves viewers wondering, Can you really *prove* love, or point to it in some way apart from what it makes people do, or not do? How we know, or show love, at least in any public kind of way, is through action—a point made by Richard Dawkins in his letter to his daughter discussed above. Likewise, with religion in the writing class, we're not looking to "prove" its existence apart from how it functions as a social, political, or psychological force. How we use it is the base from which we explore it.

As how we use it will always change, that use can be hard to identify. In identifying how we put religion to use, sometimes it's best to look for what might be called "in-between places," or hybrid areas like those cultural spaces that Homi Bhabha describes as having existed between the colonized and the settler—spaces not easily defined that give life to new mores and traditions which shape the world that we live in today. As Bhabha writes in *The Location of Culture*, we

> need to think beyond narratives of originary and initial subjectivities and to focus on those moments or processes that are produced in the articulation of cultural differences. These "in-between" spaces provide the terrain for elaborating strategies of selfhood—singular or communal— that initiate new signs of identity, and innovative sites of collaboration, and contestation, in the act of defining the idea of society itself [1–2].

Focusing on action, usefulness, and the tangible consequences of religion in the writing class helps us to see such "in-between spaces" where we might "initiate new signs of identity" and "innovative sites of collaboration" and "contestation." There's a short story by William Saroyan that I think offers one poetic, pragmatic illustration of such a space. At the end of "Resurrection of a Life," we find the narrator, who moves and sells and lives as war rages in Europe, "in the basement of a little church, deep in the shadow of faith, and of no faith: I cannot believe, it is too monstrous: where is the God of whom they speak, where?" (166). In the very last paragraph, he says,

> All that I have learned is that we breathe, from moment to moment, now, always now, and then we remember ... and all that I know is that we are somehow alive, all of us in the light, making shadows, the sun overhead, space all around us, inhaling, exhaling ... and all that I know is that I am alive and glad to be of this ugliness and this glory, somehow glad that I can remember, somehow remember the boy climbing the fig tree, unpraying but religious with joy [167].

Based on life in the here and now, "always now," Saroyan invites us to grapple with phrases like "unpraying but religious with joy," "the shadow of faith, and of no faith," and the possibility of other seemingly incongruent ideas that inhabit in-between terrain where fresh thinking and writing may be produced.

F. Scott Fitzgerald once said, "The test of a first-rate intelligence is the ability to hold two opposing ideas in the mind at the same time, and still retain the ability to function. One should, for example, be able to see that things are hopeless and yet be determined to make them otherwise" (139). For the purposes of encouraging students to look with a balanced perspective on the social possibilities of religion, we can help them develop the ability to see how religion does both good and evil simultaneously by remembering Fitzgerald's advice that the single-mindedness of insisting on *either* one choice *or* another may not be as smart as the more complex ability of being able to see at once the two sides in balance.

One text that invites us to take Fitzgerald's test is the popular film version of John Grisham's book *A Time to Kill.* Religious belief is not a dominant theme in the movie, but one sequence of scenes proves productive for our purposes. It is set in the South, where a young white lawyer tries to defend a black man for murdering the two white Klans-men who raped his daughter. About halfway through the film, in the span of less than thirty seconds, we see the Ku Klux Klan members attending their church service; this scene changes abruptly to the lawyer and his family attending their church service; then it cuts to the spirited singing of the black family in their church. There is, as one might imag-ine, an undercurrent of bitterness and self-righteousness in the first church, of formality and propriety in the next, and of transcendence and endurance in the third. Students can easily engage in discussions of the filmmaker's intent in this juxtaposition, of the fairness and point of his portrayals of the congregations, and of the varied, not-so-subtle messages that religion is called upon to validate. With this in mind, one question to ask is: "What does religious belief do in this movie?"

We can use this movie in conjunction with other works that deal with race to explore the role religious belief has played during the abo-lition movement or the civil rights movement. We might certainly work with Martin Luther King, Jr., who I discussed above, or we might work with someone like Frederick Douglass. For example, taken together, Douglass' *Narrative* and his "Fourth of July" speech provide us with some interesting material. At the end of Chapter 5 in his *Narrative*, Dou-glass describes his response to the "remarkable" circumstances sur-rounding his escape from slavery:

> I may be deemed superstitious, and even egotistical, in regarding this event as a special interposition of divine Providence in my favor. But I should be false to the earliest sentiments of my soul, if I suppressed the opinion. I prefer to be true to myself, even at the hazard of incur-ring the ridicule of others, rather than be false, and incur my own abhorrence.... [I]n the darkest hours of my career in slavery, this liv-ing word of faith and spirit of hope departed not from me, but remained like ministering angels to sheer me through the gloom. This good spirit was from God, and to him I offer thanksgiving and praise [56].

Seven years after writing these words, he writes the following in his famous "Fourth of July Speech": "Albert Barnes but uttered what the common sense of every man at all observant of the actual state of the case will receive as truth, when he declared that 'there is no power out of the church that could sustain slavery an hour, if it were not sustained in it'" (Bizzell and Herzberg 225). How might we account for these seemingly contradictory descriptions of religion from the same person? Did he change his mind during the intervening years? Is he talking about the same thing? Might Dewey's distinction between religion as a noun and religious as an adjective apply? In the context of Douglass' work, how might such a distinction be useful? Might it still be useful today?

These many intersections of religious belief and racial relations may be so plentiful because of the centrality of both of these large themes in the history and current identity of the United States. The religiosity of the United States has frequently been documented as greater than that of any other wealthy nation, and of course slavery and its consequences in our race relations have long been an important formative influence on both the economy and character of this country's society. It should therefore not be surprising that our culture's literatures, traditions, music, film, and art provide highly productive fields to investigate the mutual impacts of race and religion. Perhaps an even more important line of inquiry would involve the influences that religion and women's studies have on each other. If race and religion are stitched together throughout the fabric of American culture, why then gender issues and religion are joined throughout the far more complex varieties of global culture. Long treated as second-class citizens by most formal religions, and historically not given the empowered voices conferred by education and political power, women have, however, expressed and preserved the deepest of spiritual experiences. From Joan of Arc and Christine de Pisan in fourteenth-century France to Mother Teresa and Flannery O'Connor in the twentieth century, female religious visionaries have argued eloquently, in word and deed, for the same rights and privileges that men receive.

Joan of Arc, of course, paid the hideous penalty of being burnt at the stake for having had the temerity of leading the French army to victory over the English. She'd been told that her God-given place was back in the small village where she was raised, but like Frederick Douglass several centuries later, she was a disenfranchised mystic who could not ignore the voices within herself that told her God's place for her was at the head of an army that would save her country. Like all other women of her time, Christine de Pisan was denied the formal education of a university because she was female, but she also had the good fortune of

116

being the daughter of a brilliant man who nurtured her mind and turned her into the first female writer to support her family with her pen. Her most famous work is *The Book of the City of Ladies* in which she reports a visitation from three spirits who bring comfort to her as she is about to despair over the injustices that women suffer. Indeed, *The City of Ladies* may be not only the first such feminist tract but possibly one of the most learned works of the Middle Ages. Both de Pisan and St. Joan are extremely popular with male and female students alike once they learn just a few details of their lives and of the strangely compelling visions that motivated them.

There are now, thankfully, thousands of formidable female writers from whom we can find powerful testimony of spiritual experience. Two such authors whose work I have juxtaposed in the composition course are Sarah Grimke and Phyllis Schlafly. In "Letters on the Equality of the Sexes and the Condition of Women," Grimke responds directly to a "Pastoral Letter" which, citing the Bible, argues that essentially "the power of woman is in her dependence" (Bizzell and Herzberg 305). Also working from the Bible, Grimke offers a different perspective, taking issue at one point with the popular tenet that women need to be protected by men. Referring to "the gentle appellation of *protection*," Grimke argues that more often than not what women "have leaned upon has proved a broken reed at best, and oft a spear" (325). Phyllis Schlafly (author of 21 books, including *Equal Pay for Unequal Work* and *A Choice Not an Echo*) disagrees vehemently. In her opposition to the Equal Rights Amendment, Schlafly argued that the ERA "would take away the 'special protection' the 'Christian tradition of chivalry' offered women—in other words, the 'right' to be 'supported and protected' by men" (Critchlow 138). One might argue that the Christian chivalry to which Schlafly refers was in its full glory about six hundred years earlier when that same code of chivalry betrayed Joan of Arc; instead of protecting her, it led her to a fiery death at the stake. In any case, composition students can consider such various positions not necessarily to choose who is right and who is wrong, but to explore in their writing the powerful influence of religious belief in these women's lives and the lives of others.

Another extraordinarily important female writer who can have great impact on student thinking about religion and its uses is the incomparable Flannery O'Connor, whose short stories take the fictional device

117

of revelation or epiphany to produce character insights that perhaps only James Joyce had been able to match. The device of revelation usually revolves around a sudden and searing insight into a spiritual or psychological phenomenon that visits the character without warning. It usually transforms the character's self-image and her/his awareness of others. In "Everything That Rises Must Converge," for instance, we find an elderly woman who has worked unstintingly and sacrificed all comforts for herself only to finance her ungrateful son's education. Now, with his newly acquired superiority, he is embarrassed by his mother, particularly when she buys and wears in public an outlandish hat that brings with it the confidence of knowing, "I at least won't meet myself coming and going" (5). But she does "meet" herself—in the person of another elderly woman who, because she is black, is clearly beneath her. Her son is cruel, even gleeful, as he spitefully tells his mother that she fully deserves her shock and humiliation. Hearing the hatred in his voice, her heart breaks and she collapses in an ugly mass on the curb of a busy street. The reader is led to believe that this old woman has had her revelation, but in fact it is the young man who suddenly and simultaneously sees that he truly loves his mother, that he has lost her forever, and that he himself is the cause of all this spiritual chaos. The moment of epiphany is shocking for both the young man and for many readers, especially those who are coming to O'Connor's work for the first time. They are led through most of the story to focus on the old woman's vanities and even to share in her son's embarrassment, but at the crucial moment of spiritual understanding O'Connor does not let her reader avoid the hard implications of what occurred. It is a powerful illustration of what the mother's religious belief and her son's belated spiritual revelation have accomplished in their lives.

Not all O'Connor's stories are so difficult to ponder, but they all turn on the fulcrum of religious or spiritual epiphany, and once students are told something about the author's own life, they surely see the connection between what religion did for O'Connor personally and how she transformed those experiences into her fiction. Some other examples that can be highly effective for student writers are O'Connor's "Greenleaf," which is ripe with the thorny crown and judgment of Jesus, or "Revelation," "Parker's Back," and "Good Country People." Each of these stories serves well to inspire strong essays about what religion can do.

Most of my students, however, seem to have particularly enjoyed "A Good Man Is Hard to Find," in which O'Connor provides a moral enforcer through the hands of a killer (not unlike the way in which Quentin Tarantino later does with Jules Winnfield in the movie *Pulp Fiction*). This character, the Misfit, is at once a cold-blooded murderer of women and children and, as Harold Bloom puts it, "an instrument of Catholic grace." It is quite a story to wrestle with, and it can be productive to play around with O'Connor's "penetrating insight that religion for her countrymen and -women [is] not the opiate, but rather the poetry of the people" (Bloom 54).

In addition to O'Connor's short stories, I've had success as well with Philip Roth ("Defender of the Faith"), Richard Wright ("Bright and Morning Star"), and Tomas Rivera ("…And the Earth Did Not Part"). I also want to recommend a novel and a play that can provide "innovative sites of collaboration and contestation," as Homi Bhabha put it, for our work with religion: Bernard Malamud's *The Fixer* and Tony Kushner's *Angels in America*. In the beginning of *The Fixer*, set in anti–Semitic Tsarist Russia, Yakov Bok responds to his stepfather's admonition "Don't forget your God!" by replying, "Who forgets who … what do I get from him but a bang on the head and a stream of piss in my face" (17). As the novel progresses, however, Yakov's "Jewishness" is increasingly thrust upon him, and, while attempting to take up Spinoza's theology, he struggles to understand what religion has done to him (and others) and what it could do for him (and others). How Yakov and his religion are eventually portrayed as inextricably bound, and how together they are ultimately understood as both *a part of* and *a consequence of* history and politics, is also particularly appealing from our lens.

Kushner's play, set in the Reagan '80s and featuring Roy Cohn, a gay couple facing AIDS, and a Mormon couple confronting drug addiction and latent homosexuality, offers a number of different characters and angles to focus upon. The social structure as well as the spiritual center of religion lie at the heart of this play, and there is an interesting theme of duality that runs throughout it, i.e., a pattern in the play whereby things usually considered as opposites are woven together, such as being both Mormon and gay, real and hallucinatory, tragic and comic, political and personal, a character and an archetype, a "sinner" seduced by angels, and so on. The way in which the play ultimately depicts a

Godless heaven and a God who can be sued for abandonment also fits into this same pattern and provides us ample material to work with regarding our underlying focus on mediation, hybridity, and human action. In addition, both Malamud's novel and Kushner's play have been made into movies which can serve as useful compliments.

Working with Art

Like many composition teachers, I've asked my students at one time or another to write about art. Sometimes, the art that students write about has something to do with religion, or the student interprets a piece of art in overtly religious terms. What has helped me to frame this assignment is a book by Sylvan Barnet called *A Short Guide to Writing About Art*. In this book, Barnet offers some "theories of value" that often serve as a basis when responding to art. Here is the list that he provides:

1. Truth
2. Instrumental Value (or Utility)
3. Ideology
4. Intrinsic Aesthetic Merit
5. Expressiveness
6. Sincerity
7. Technique
8. Originality
9. Historical Importance

I include the entire list because most of them (if not all of them) illustrate places we either should or should not go with religion in the composition class.

Barnet briefly discusses each of the nine, and it becomes clear rather quickly that we may want to avoid, for example, number one and number three. Regarding Truth, Barnet writes that "at its simplest, perhaps, this means that art should present images that closely resemble ... the world around us" (229). In other words, art should represent the way the world is, or the way we see it *to be*. It represents what is True. We move in a similar direction with Ideology, where one is inclined to argue "that a work embodying such-and-such ideas is (depending on the critics own ideology) good or bad" (230). Operating under these theories of value—Truth and Ideology—it is easy to see how students may end up saying things like "the light in this painting is God's infinite grace and wisdom" or "this piece of art shows that God is a myth and a killer." In my experience, this road can be rough as we're led by the wrong verb.

By highlighting others from Barnet's list, however, we can move from "is" to "does." Number two, for instance: Instrumental Value (or Utility). Here we look to "something outside of the work itself, something *extrinsic* to the work." He adds that critics "who hold this position say that a good work of art has *instrumental value*; the work is an *instrument*, improving us spiritually or morally, or giving us insight into the political system so that we can work for a more just system" (230). Such a view moves us to consider what a piece of art might do for us collectively, or how it prompts us to act, or the consequences it provokes in the real world. As does Technique, number seven on the list. Here we are asked to consider the effect of an artist's skill as opposed to arriving at certain Truths about the world. Barnet notes that in "valuing technique (skillful execution) we may, when speaking of paintings, be getting back to realism: 'Look how the painter has caught the texture of fur here, and the texture of silk there. And just look at the light reflecting on that glass of wine!'" (233–34). We can, for our purposes, think of realism here in the way that Joyce Carol Oates once defined it: "to be a realist (in art or in life) is to acknowledge that all things might be other than they are" (555).

In addition, when working with art we can prompt students to try to consider how a particular artist or particular piece portrays or occupies that in-between space where fresh meaning can be made when it comes to God and science. To put it another way, we can draw on John Dewey and ask students how a piece of art may provoke a religious experience without being rooted in religion—that is, without being based on a supernatural tradition. We might look to the work of James Turrell as one example.

It's been said that to see Turrell's art, "you must first become hopelessly lost" (Hylton 37). Turrell works a lot with lighting and open spaces; his incomplete masterpiece is, in fact, a huge crater of an old volcano in Arizona. One piece that was shown in Los Angeles was described like this: "The room was devoid of boundaries, just an eternity of inky blackness, with the outline of a huge lavender rectangle floating in the distance, and beyond it the tall plane of green light stretching toward an invisible horizon, where it dissolved into a crimson stripe" (36). The effect of Turrell's work often is, to put it mildly, disorienting. As Wil Hylton writes, "Not everyone enjoys the Turrell experience. It requires a degree of surrender. There is a certain comfort in knowing what is real and where things are; to have that comfort stripped away can be rapturous, or distressing" (37). Stripping away such comfort is what Ann Berthoff speaks of when it comes to the value of chaos and imagination at the beginning of the writing process.

In addition to Dewey and Berthoff, Turrell's work reminds us of William James as well with respect to knowledge *a priori*. Like many artists, Turrell himself doesn't know what he is going to do until he does it—a disconcerting trait for those attempting to show his work. In Seattle, for instance, he was asked for months how he planned to finish a project, and his only answer was "I don't know." Just before it was slated to open, he came up with the following: "rectangular windows [that] exploded with brilliant light: an ethereal pink on the left, and a deep blue on the right, and in the middle a mélange of both colors that Andrews [the curator] still can't quite explain. 'I can really only describe it as fog,' he said. 'These two extraordinary colors moved toward each other and through each other, and it was just crazy'" (58). Turrell was able to sculpt the science of light to produce a surreal effect. Or, one could argue, a religious experience—an experience that brought together two different, brilliant colors.

Writing Assignments

In this section I refer to ten student essays; five of these appear as full texts for further exploration in the Appendix. These essays all come from my first-year composition courses except one Response Essay, which comes from a sophomore-level English course. In all, I address three Personal Narratives, four Persuasive Essays, and three Response Essays. I offer these essays as examples of how some of my students have actually written about religion, and I comment and make suggestions based on the approach I've tried to describe in this book. I do not comment on mechanics, grammar, or sentence structure; I focus only on content and the gist of their argument, response, or narrative. A summary of each assignment to which students responded appears in the Appendix (these assignments should sound familiar to anyone who teaches composition). I want to note that all of these students chose to write on religion. I use their essays with permission, and I have deleted their names for the sake of anonymity.

"Remove 'Under God?'" In this persuasive essay, my student argues that the words "Under God" should not be removed from the Pledge of Allegiance. She provides some history on when and how the words were added, and, in the first couple of pages, argues that the purpose of adding these words was to provide the United States with a more particular identity and help it stand out from other countries. Throughout her essay the author argues that if ours is a representative democracy and most people in the country still believe in God, the addition of these words to the Pledge should not disturb or agitate nonbelievers. These arguments are effective and well supported.

Her position then changes course, however, and she begins to make unsupported ontological claims, such as "If He is removed, the country will fall apart" (she makes this claim at least twice). She also generally argues that the United States was founded on "belief in God" and asks, "Why would you want to remove the very thing our country was founded on?" She cites, too, someone who states that "this country was 'born under God.'" At this point, many teachers, including myself, might suggest in the margin something like "consider your audience" or "support these claims—not all will take these statements as fact." But such comments do not go far enough; the student may simply say to herself, "I did consider my audience—*everyone* needs to know this. It's true." And this is where we can bring the student back inside our pragmatic boundaries, by steering her away from making such Truth claims in the first place and urging her towards describing what would actually happen to people in the country if we were to take that phrase out of the Pledge of Allegiance. Or, conversely, what does it do for us, practically speaking, while it's in there? If she continued along those initial lines of how it sets us apart from other countries and why that is a good thing, her essay would have been stronger.

As she concludes, the author offers some practical advice, suggesting that those who are offended can choose not to say the Pledge (or choose to tell children not to say it). She then adds, however, that God "gives people the choice. They can choose to believe; or they can choose to reject. The person just must take the consequences of their choice, good or bad." Her reference here seems to be to the reality of heaven or hell waiting for those of us who choose accordingly—a reference that is difficult to make and support in our classroom. She ends her essay with the following two sentences: "God reigns in our lives and in our country whether we see it or not. 'Under God' should not be removed." These are the kinds of statements we can nudge students away from by creating an environment where we focus on the palpable consequences of religious belief in society—which this author does in many ways—rather than ironclad assertions about the nature of God. Admittedly, this is hard to do. As Dewey and James have noted, religion is saturated with emotional elements—most people, one way or the other, are invested, which can make for some great writing, but can also lead us astray. And to complicate matters, in the first-year composition course students are often attempting to express their complicated thoughts on this subject in a formal piece of writing for the very first time.

"The Downside of Religion" The full text of this persuasive essay may be found in the Appendix. The author largely follows our pragmatic track by addressing what religion does in the world, but the title is a bit misleading as it discusses the good that religion does as well. The introductory paragraph ends by stating that religion "has slowed down man's progress, and also it has caused many conflicts and wars." A couple paragraphs later, the author then describes the good it can do: "There are many upsides to religion, and reasons why it is very good for people to believe in something." We then swing back to the harm that religion can do, with historical references and quotes from people like Mohandas Gandhi that paint religious belief in a negative light. The author is clearly attempting to negotiate the conflicting consequences of religious belief.

In trying to strike a balance, or find a harmony of sorts, this author cites the theory of Theistic Evolution, the belief that God guides the process of evolution. She also offers the following from Albert Einstein: "Science without religion is lame; religion without science is blind." The controversy over stem cell research is presented as well in neutral terms, and the essay ends by stating that religion will always be around—a conclusion that can be reasonably drawn from what precedes it, despite being a bit general and disconnected from the title. While the author is careful to avoid any self-serving ontological claims, I invite the reader to think about how this author might improve her essay. She is working hard to pull together the good and the bad that religious belief does in the world, but what suggestions might you make regarding her conclusion, or her ultimate argument?

"Morals in Modern Life" The full text of this persuasive essay may be found in the Appendix. The essay begins with several thoughtful questions, and leads the reader in the direction of how religion is useful in helping society function. The author then begins to argue that while religious belief can provide a moral framework, it is not the source of morality. As social creatures, the author suggests, humans have developed a sense of morality that may, in different ways, be developed and disseminated by religious institutions, but "just as the schools themselves do not invent or discover the knowledge they impart on students, neither did religions invent the moral compass."

The author of this essay continues to ask questions as a way to argue that things like self-preservation and the family unit have had the most to do with providing for us a moral code. Without denigrating religious belief, she focuses on how such belief prompts, for example, random acts of kindness, and supports her findings with tangible evidence. The author looks at action in the world to support her thesis, and while she could have incorporated and addressed more evidence to the contrary, she steers clear of what is True or Untrue and concentrates on how religious belief squares with our other ideas for constructing and maintaining a democratic society.

The concluding paragraph begins with "Clearly though religions teach morality, they are not the source of them." A sense of morality, she concludes, comes from our interactions with one another, interactions that include but are not limited to or rooted in religion. The author's focus is, for the most part, on action and consequence in a social setting, rather than on the inherent moral nature of religious belief. Having said that, I again invite the reader to think about where this author could strengthen her argument given this kind of assignment and our particular framework?

"One Nation, Under God" In this persuasive essay, my student begins by referring to the founding of the United States, our freedom to worship god, and the statement in the Declaration of Independence that men "are endowed by their Creator." The author notes that "Creator" is capitalized, that Jefferson did not say here something vague like "a higher power," and that Creator "indeed is referring to the one and only God." The essay then moves to how and why a national religion was not established by the founders. His arguments here are persuasive. At this point, however, we see an abrupt shift, as the author starts a new paragraph and states, "I believe that everyone should convert to Christianity." The reader is not shown, however, what such a conversion would necessarily do for us in the world. Rather, the author writes that all should convert to Christianity because things are bad right now. He argues, "Look at the state of our economy, look at the news...." There is, however, little discussion of how converting to Christianity would help our economy. Perhaps it would. Perhaps that might be a tangible effect of converting, and if so, that is the argument that needs to be made to strengthen this essay.

Because of that shift to conversion, the central claim of the essay becomes a little hard to follow. There is, midway, some discussion on the differences between Protestants and Roman Catholics, and then the statement, "Now this is really biased, but although not everyone believes in the one true God, they really should." The author notes how certain religious institutions can cause harm in the world (specifically regarding homosexuality), but we quickly move again to the following: "Look at the state of our economy, look at the news." The final paragraph begins with "...our nation is in distress. There are so many things wrong with society today as far as morality is concerned along with all of our nation's economic state." The essay concludes that a "return to what the Pilgrims originally wanted for this country is what we need to turn our nation around, not a new deal, not a better president, a return to God."

The essay is passionate and strong in many ways, but it ultimately argues that because the world is in bad shape, we should choose Christianity. The author, however, offers little evidence of human action in the world to support that assertion. Had he done so, the essay would have been a lot stronger, and he may have been more likely to avoid isolated, ontological claims that are often seen as only serving themselves.

Untitled In an untitled response essay, one of my students responded to "A City of Churches" by Donald Barthelme. My student positions himself as a devout Christian, and states that his central aim is to suggest that "nobody should be judged by his or her religion." He sets his sights on how a particular culture will influence the practice of Christianity. He applies this thinking to Barthelme's story, and argues that Mr. Philips and other characters who live in Prester are "abusing religion, taking it to a whole new level, and making it appalling." He states that "their actions towards Cecelia" end up taking "away this girl's life by forcing her to stay and work at Prester."

There is a lot of emphasis in this essay on action, and how people "practice their faith." The author incorporates his own experience growing up a Christian in Malaysia, where most people are Buddhist or Muslim, and remembers how he "was often made fun of in class that Jesus was not real." He avoids this debate himself, and tries instead to explore "the creative ways in which religions of the region [Asia] are responding to natural, social, and global stressors." He repeats that where we come from will affect how we practice our faith, and says that mistakes will be made: "nobody is perfect." His point on perfection is a reference to "A City of Churches." He quotes Mr. Philips ("We want you standing behind the counter of the car-rental agency, during regular business hours. It will make the town complete.") and notes that "The people of Prester are using religion as a weapon of unity … to make their town complete and more perfect."

Near the end of the essay, the author brings up Sigmund Freud as an example of an atheist. While this paragraph could have used some more revision, the author clearly tries to get at the tangible consequences of religious belief: He states that to Freud, "religion is a safety net to guide powerless beings through rough patches." In coming back to the townsfolk in Barthelme's story, the author writes that "their action in forcing the girl to fulfill an imaginary quota violates every Bible teaching" and that "their actions go against … respecting someone as an equal." He concludes that "To a certain extent, religious beliefs motivate a person to act in a certain direction."

The last two sentences of the essay are a good stab at exploring that vital link between belief and worldly acts: "…religion is an entity that has to be fully understood and not forced upon. If it is not practiced in one's daily life, it will never be an accurate reflection of one's doing." How it is practiced, or what it does in the world, is at the heart of this student's essay.

Untitled In another untitled response essay, one of my students writes that many of the stories we read in class offered a "negative depiction of religion." He responds to three stories in particular: "The German Refugee" by Bernard Malamud, "Death of a Favorite" by J. F. Powers, and "Defender of the Faith" by Philip Roth. He writes that "Religion was used in these stories as the force for evil rather than good. There was a Jew that gases himself to death after fleeing for his life, a Jewish trainee and Sergeant that use their faith as a disguise, and a cat that is tortured and ultimately killed by a couple of priests." While this may be an oversimplified view of religion in these stories, his central point is that too often what gets highlighted in our culture is the negative rather than the positive that religion does in the world.

Making a connection between morality and religion, the author writes in particular that "It appears to me that many people want to push us away from believing." He implies that this push has led to an increase in selfish, destructive behavior, and that a negative focus on religious belief only makes all of us more cynical and isolated. He cites specific examples of bad acts by religious figures, noting that these are the stories that make the news, "but we rarely see any stories of the positives that people are doing around the world." He asks, "how often is it reported what the local churches are doing for the community, or the projects that they are involved in around the world?" and he suggests that "we work together to report, and follow the positives of life, instead of drowning ourselves with the horrors of men."

In response to the negativity he sees as so often ascribed to religion, the author taps into what his own religious belief has done for him. "If I were to write a story that was centered on my faith," he says, "I would have shown struggles, but also display how the strength of my faith helped in triumphing over the struggles." Negativity breeds negativity, he suggests, and what we need is the opposite—a positive understanding, or at least a more balanced understanding of religious belief that might lead to more positive deeds in the world. Or, as he puts it in his final sentence that could also be taken as a shot at his teacher, "We were fed stories filled with destruction when in reality this world needs a group hug." As I mentioned to this author, the central aim of his paper is strong and well supported— religious belief certainly does a lot of good in the world, and the more we focus on the good that it does, the more good we will probably see, and do.

"The Bible's Influence on the Founding of the United States" The full text of this response essay can be found in the Appendix. As the title suggests, the focus of this essay is on the role religious belief played in forming the country. The writer states that obviously "not all the founders were practicing Christians," but argues that the framers of the United States drew a great deal from Christian principles. He first cites the phrase from the Declaration of Independence that "all men are created equal" and notes that this does not mean that all men are created equal when it comes to physical strength, or intellectual ability, or moral inclination. It does not mean that all men "behave equally well," he writes, "but their lives have a moral worth no greater or less than anyone else." The author argues that the "concept that every life has equal value was at the time a uniquely Christian idea," noting that the "Bible states that every human life is of infinite value to God and that he loves everyone equally." He specifically cites Galatians 3:28: "There is neither Jew nor Greek, there is neither slave nor free, there is no male and female, for you are all one in Christ Jesus."

The author writes that the idea of protecting individual rights in this regard is rooted in Christianity, and that when Jefferson said that such rights were "self-evident" it was because they were in agreement with the laws of nature. "The idea of an innate natural law," says the author, "is a biblical concept." He supports this assertion in several ways, and then moves on to his second central example of Biblical influence on the founding of the United States: the system of checks and balances. He says that this system was a bold affirmation of "the founders' belief in the Biblical principle that human beings are members of a fallen and sinful race.... The assumption," he adds, "that no man deserves absolute power over his fellow countrymen due to his fallen and sinful nature led to the idea for the separation of powers and the doctrine of checks and balances."

The author of this essay notes a number of times that the founders drew from lots of different places when forming the country, but argues that "they depended on the principles found in the Bible to a large degree." He is careful not to argue for the essential goodness of Biblical influence, but suggests that without that influence our laws and our country "would surely be very different." As with all the full texts that appear in the appendix, I invite the reader to think about the strengths of this essay in light of the pragmatic lens of this book and, in the same light, where the author might work to improve his argument.

"Religion in My Life" The full text of this personal narrative can be found in the Appendix. The author begins by noting that the topic is popular and divisive and acknowledges that there are "multiple sides" to consider. He states at the outset as well that his own experience has brought about a change: "my perspective has swayed from time to time as I have learned to take a broader view." He recounts his abrupt childhood introduction to religion, noting that he and his siblings felt like they were "being indoctrinated" and "forced to follow their [parents'] path." He notes, however, that now as an adult and a father, he holds no grudges. He believes in God, and encourages his children to keep an open mind, letting them choose for themselves what they want to believe.

The author touches a couple of times on the idea that experience can bring about change ("my perspective on religion has changed as I have grown older," for instance). He seems, as well, to draw a rather Deweyan distinction between religion as a static noun and religious as a more fluid adjective: "I also believe that it is not necessary for an individual to attend church three or even seven days a week to show that they believe in God or to be considered religious." He cites a current example of harmful religious behavior in his opinion (members of the Westboro Baptist Church picketing military funerals) and comes back to the importance of experience. "For me," he says, referring to his upbringing, "the first-hand experience was necessary so I could be better informed to understand religion and pass that on to my children and respect the positions of others on the subject."

Throughout this essay, the author seems interested in how we respond to our individual encounters with religious belief and how that response can change and influence our behavior. He ends by referring again to the way in which religion tends to engender division, and invites the reader to think back on his narrative as one way to bridge that divide.

"Man in the Middle" In this personal narrative, my student structures his essay by describing where religious belief has placed him in the world, or where he sees himself in relation to religion. That place is in the middle, trying to listen to all sides. He begins with some effective rhetorical questions based on how he has come to arrive at his own particular beliefs, and then he moves in a practical direction by asking how religious belief connects or disconnects people in the world. He suggests a focus on what works in our lives to help us find peace, and in arguing for tolerance, he writes that "another way to look at faiths, beliefs and religions is to imagine them all as spokes of a giant wheel. Not one spoke can be longer than another, nor can a spoke be missing for the wheel to spin properly."

He also asks what religion is, and answers that it "is simply a structure of outlined beliefs that serves as guidance on how to live and in some cases how to get to heaven." I remember asking him to think about how those belief structures might change over the years, and how being "in the middle" might help negotiate that change. Moving in that direction, he highlights the importance of remembering that we will never be able to fully see what others see, and that others will never be able to see fully what we see. What must remain constant, he argues, is an emphasis on communication, community, and peace. To conclude, he uses the image of a man in the middle to demonstrate the tension and friction associated with the position he proposes; he seems to imply that such a strain is necessary and often fruitful.

"Finding God: My Life Story" The full text of this personal narrative can be found in the Appendix. In the Introduction to this book I refer to Thomas Deans who has recently argued that the composition canon should include more primary sacred texts. The personal narrative I include here is a good example of how students already draw upon and include such texts in their writing, and thus, I believe, an example which supports Deans' proposal. As students already turn to primary sacred texts, if we were to invite and validate their usage within the pragmatic boundaries I sketch in this book, we would be in a better position to help students incorporate them more fully and effectively in their writing.

The author of this narrative has based his essay on some very specific tenets from the Bible. In the body of his essay he describes how coming to Christianity affected his life for the better, but he does not weave those specific tenets throughout his writing. Instead, he lists them separately at the end. As he worked on this essay, I told him that he was more than welcome to cite directly from the Bible in support of his essay, but I don't think he was ever convinced that the Bible was a valid academic source, even in a personal narrative. At the end of his essay, he puts the crucial tenets in bold to highlight how important they are, but the effect, in my opinion, is to further separate them from the rest of his essay. It is also not completely clear why these particular tenets were chosen.

The essay is powerful in many ways, but it might be stronger had those biblical passages been incorporated throughout. My guess is that if as a field we started to send a stronger signal that such texts may be included as valuable sources of knowledge (as Thomas Deans suggests), students like the author here would work with them more comfortably and productively throughout their writing. I invite the reader to look at the full text in the appendix and to think about how this author could have included those passages throughout his essay. How could he have specifically connected them to points in his story? How might they be explored more fully to strengthen his story?

In discussing these essays, I've tried to illustrate some of the ways students work within the boundaries I've sketched in this book regarding religion, and also where we might attempt to steer writers back when they move to places not quite suited for the composition class. I want to thank my students for having the courage to write about this topic, which is not easy to do. And I want to thank them for letting me use their work in this book.

By the end of William James' *The Varieties of Religious Experience*, James seems to conclude that having such a variety in the world does, for the most part, sort itself out in a positive way. He notes, "Each attitude being a syllable in human nature's total message, it takes the whole of us to spell the meaning out completely" (420). To conclude this chapter on assignments, I suggest that we ask our students to grapple with James' position here in conjunction with John Updike's 2002 short story which bears the same title, "Varieties of Religious Experience." Updike's story depicts one man's struggle with God in the wake of the September 11 terrorist attacks; it also focuses on two of the terrorists, one of the victims, and the plane that ultimately crashed in Pennsylvania. This story appears to suggest a different conclusion than the one James draws—having so many different religious beliefs in the world might not, in fact, be such a good thing. As our students think and write in response to these possibilities, we can remind them that—as both James and Updike would say—it's not the right answer we're after so much. It's the way we wrestle with the topic.

Conclusion

Religion belongs in the first-year composition course. In fact, as Mark Edmundson says, "Religion is the right place to start [any] humanities course, for a number of reasons, even if what we're going on to do is to read the novels of Henry James" (25). Disappointed with his student evaluations in that they reflected mostly how well his students were being entertained as opposed to how well they were being challenged to think, reflect, and create, Edmundson started asking his students at the University of Virginia what they thought about God. He did so to get them to think of things that really matter, like who we are and what we should be doing with our lives. Working with religion, he felt, would help students construct their final narratives, a phrase he takes from Richard Rorty that "involves the ultimate set of terms that we use to confer value on experience … where our principles are manifest" (25). He draws as well on Emerson's essay "Circles" to show that these Final Narratives are never quite final, but subject to change as they ceaselessly ripple outward "to new and larger circles" (29). Edmundson suggests that "we might think of the question about religion as a way to tap into one's ultimate terms, to make contact with one's outer-lying circles, and in so doing initiate the process of growth" (31).

In a likely reference to William James' talk of living and dead options, Edmundson laments that most "professors of the humanities have little interest in religion as a field of live options" as most have long since developed a secular view of the world or have decided it's best to keep their religious beliefs "separate from their pedagogy" (28). But, as many scholars in the field of composition and rhetoric have argued, Edmundson writes that the "question of belief matters greatly to the young" and that "asking it can break through the ideologies of training and entertaining" (28). In part it can do so by disrupting a culture that suggests everything is easy and pre-packaged, where important issues have long been settled and what's left is superficial show, a culture that Edmundson says universities themselves help to create by sinking money into things like recreation centers instead of education. He writes that teachers "need to provide a scene where not-knowing is, at least at the outset, valued more than full, worldly confidence. Thoreau heading to Walden Pond almost empty handed, Emily Dickinson going up to her room in Amherst to engage in a solitary dialogue with God" (35). Teachers can set that scene by opening the door to religion.

Religion, of course, is already there, waiting for the invitation. With respect to writing teachers at her university in Oklahoma, Priscilla Perkins observed that "as careful as they were to cordon off all Bible talk, students still found opportunities to bring it in to their classrooms" (587). My own experience has told me the same, and that we need to address it further. Elizabeth Vander Lei writes that "by negotiating religious faith in our composition classrooms, we better teach our students how to analyze and respond to the arguments they encounter every day in political speeches, civic debate, and scholarly discussions" (6). The method I've sketched is an attempt to help guide that negotiation. As a method only, Loren Macdonald concluded more than a century ago that this pragmatic approach to religion has no design other than to find "life's right proportion and harmony" (26). To help illustrate, Macdonald writes, "If the leader of an orchestra should find that the player on the clarinet, in his eagerness to add to the music, was asserting exclusive rights, and drowning out all the other instruments, he would endeavor to set that particular player right with respect to the total harmony" (26). The pragmatic method, says Macdonald, claims

> that the best music comes from the full orchestra, each instrument joining with the others in perfect harmony. But the truth? you say. Well, tested by life, the music of the full orchestra is the truth and there is no other. Let us wait. Doubtless the clarinet player will discover himself some day that his instrument alone fails to produce the total grand effect [27].

Today, many in secular composition classes across the country worship God and faithfully go to church, while many others do not. The pragmatists provide a map for pulling us together and striking the right note when working with religion in the first-year writing course.

Appendix: Student Essays

In "Writing Assignments" near the end of Chapter 4, I discuss a number of student essays that I have received over the years in the first-year composition course (and one essay I received in a sophomore-level English course). In this appendix, I include the full text of five of those essays. The essays came in response to three different writing assignments: Personal Narrative, Persuasive Essay, and Response Essay. I offer the entire text of these essays here so that the reader may more fully appreciate the students' objectives and how they tried to reach those objectives. I also invite the reader to ask herself—given the particular assignment—how she would respond to these essays. More specifically, how does the pragmatic bend put forth in this book become evident through these examples of student writing, and how might that particular bend guide any advice the reader may have for the students to improve their papers? In asking these questions, it may be helpful to revisit my comments on these essays in the "Writing Assignments" section in Chapter 4.

I have made very few changes to the original versions of these essays. My purpose is to focus on substance rather than mechanics, so I have left most grammar and MLA citation errors as they originally appeared. A synopsis of each assignment precedes the essays which were written for that assignment.

Persuasive Essay Assignment

For this assignment, students were asked to choose a topic under the broad heading of "Negotiating Difference." They had to make an argument—to persuade the reader to think a certain way or act a certain way with respect to their topic. They had to support their position with various examples and at least three outside sources. The particular approach was up to them, but they were to think about some of the different arguments we had read and talked about in class, and to consider Aristotle's rhetorical triangle (logos, ethos, pathos) in establishing their position. They were encouraged to pick a topic they were interested in, and to draw on their own experiences. They were not required to write on religion.

Persuasive Essay #1

The Downside of Religion

Religion is a very popular, controversial subject that is argued about all throughout the world. There are many different beliefs as to what the higher power is, or what to believe in. Different cultures have different beliefs, and grow up with different religions. Even though religion provides people with answers they would like to have, it has also created many problems all throughout the world. It has protests against science because it is not what some religions agree with, so it has slowed down man's progress, and also it has caused many conflicts and wars.

There are numerous ways to describe or explain religion. Religion is defined as a set of beliefs concerning the cause, nature, and purpose of the universe, especially when considered as the creation of the superhuman agency or agencies, usually involving devotional or ritual observances, and often containing a moral code governing the conduct of human affairs (dictionary.com). Many religions give people something to believe in, like the meaning of life or even hope in an afterlife. All religions are in some cases similar, but are also very different. They seem to help people have morals, to help people do the right thing, seeing as humans usually can't do that on their own. However, there are some people that will never have the right morals.

As of right now, the top five largest religions start with Christianity, which includes around 2.1 billion people, and 33.0 percent of the world. The second is Islam at 1.3 billion people, and 20.1 percent of the world. The third is Hinduism, which includes 851 million people and 13.3 percent of the world; fourth is Buddhism at 375 million people, and 5.9 percent of the world. The final on the list is Sikhism, which includes 25 million people and 0.4 percent of the world (Pearson Education).

There are many upsides to religion, and reasons why it is very good for people to believe in something. For one, it gives people hope, faith, and correct morals to do well in their life. By giving you good morals, it makes you believe in some cultures that you will be saved, or in Christianity you won't go to hell. This helps to have fewer murders and less wrongdoing. Without some sort of backbone or structure, murder might be a bigger problem in society than it already is (it may not be as big of a deal to people, and it wouldn't be frowned upon as much). Also, when you go to churches, temples, etc., you will be able to interact with others of the same cultures and views; it helps the people feel unity. It helps bring people together and make people happy. When you believe or have faith, you feel as if you have a purpose in life, or a sense of direction.

There are some reasons as to why people believe that religion could be wrong, or pointless. Some people believe it is wrong because they say it brainwashes its worshipers, and also uses fear tactics in order to keep people in line. For example, in Christianity if you do wrong, you are threatened with going to hell. It also has a part in slowing man's progress, like when scientists do stem cell research; religious figures protest and become extremely upset. Different religious views can cause problems such as war, and it has been a problem in every time period. There have been wars such as the Crusades and the Thirty Years War. Some religions are against gay marriage and also put down abortions. They seem to not want people to have their own mind and point of views. The theory of evolution is basically hidden from children out of respect for the church's oppositions.

A religious war is caused by differences in religion. According to a Wikipedia article on Religious War, a religious war can involve one state with an established religion against another state with a different religion or a different sect within the same religion, or a religiously motivated group attempting to spread its faith by violence, or to suppress another group because of its religious beliefs. A few wars recorded in history were the Crusades, The Muslim conquests, the French Wars of Religion, Thirty Years War, and the Reconquista. Some wars that are considered religious ones have other reasons also, such as political or economic reasons. Usually in these kinds of wars, places that are used for worship are destroyed in order to weaken the opposing side (this, of course, can happen if the war is religious or not). "The most heinous and the most cruel crimes of which history has record have been committed under the cover of religion or equally noble motives," as Mahatma Gandhi put it.

The Crusades is an example of a war that was caused because of different opinions in religion. They were a series of wars started by Europe against the Saracens, which was the word they used to use to describe a Moslem during these times. They initiated in 1095 when Pope Claremont declared the first one to start. The war was centered on the City of Jerusalem, which held significance for the Christian religion. The nations of Europe were trying to rescue the holy places from the Mohammedans. There were nine wars total and over a span of 200 years there was almost constant fighting. The positive factor from this war was it helped progress civilization in this time; It helped political matters, and it also prompted the discovery voyages.

The Thirty Years War was a conflict between the Protestants and Catholics of the Christian religion which lasted from 1618 to 1648. Most of the fighting happened within the German States, but it spread through almost all of Europe. This brought much famine and sickness throughout these countries. Ferdinand II inherited the Bohemian throne and was the heir to the Holy Roman Empire, which caused this war. This caused the Protestants to rebel. This war went through four different phases, which was the Bohemian Revolt, Danish Intervention, Swedish Intervention, and finally the French Intervention. A treaty was negotiated called the Peace of Westphalia, but the actual treaty that ended this war was the Treaty of Munster in 1648. This war caused people to divide their loyalties between religion and country.

Another major religious issue is the theory of evolution. In today's world, it's very hard to find a scientist that doesn't believe evolution has existed. The theory was created by Charles Darwin in 1859, and he described that creatures evolve over time through "natural selection." This means that animals and plants change by adapting to their environments over time. This theory has scientific evidence to prove it. According to National Geographic, about 13.7 billion years ago the universe was formed, and the earth was formed around 4.7 billion years ago. Humans only have existed for a hundred thousand years or so. Many people who believe in God do not believe this can be true, seeing as this was not at all stated in the Bible. In the Old Testament of the Bible, the book of Genesis explains how they believe the Earth actually formed, and how everything was created. They have no need for any type of scientific proof because they go by faith. This is the theory of creationism. Opinions vary between the different kinds of religions, but this is just an example. There is, however, a theory of Theistic Evolution, and this has been a more recent view from some religious groups, including the Catholic Church. They believe that God guides the process of evolution. Or as Albert Einstein stated, "Science without religion is lame; religion without science is blind."

A controversy that is an issue in the United States today is whether stem cell research and cloning should be accepted by people. Most religious and also some other people take the pro-life stand on this subject, and believe this is against our morals as human beings. They believe that this is considered the same as an abortion, and is against the ways of God. They consider them alive because they still have DNA. Taking the embryo from the human and extracting the cells are what they consider murdering a human, even though it is not yet alive. There are so many reasons as to why it is important that we can study what we can do with stem cells, for this could even be part of the cure for cancer or other life-threatening illnesses. Scientists want to test these cells because they could treat certain diseases like diabetes and heart disease.

Religion will always be one of the main ways of life, and bring people faith and happiness. It will also cause us problems, as seen in the past. No matter what happens, it will always be practiced and followed by the people that have faith in what they believe in.

Works Cited

"The Crusades." *The Middle Ages*. Web. 1 Aug. 2012.

Lovgren, Stefan. "Evolution and Religion Can Coexist, Scientists Say." *National Geographic*. National Geographic Society, 18 Oct. 2004. Web. 04 Aug. 2012.

Masci, David, ed. "Darwin Debated: Religion vs. Evolution." *Pew Research*. Pew Research Center, 4 Feb. 2009. Web. 31 July 2012.

"Pros and Cons of Religion." *KeyFrame5*. KeyFrame5 Studios, 2011. Web. 31 July 2012.

"Religion." Dictionary.com, LLC, 2012. Web. 31 July 2012.

"Religion." *Wikipedia*. 29 July 2012. Web. 1 Aug. 2012.

"Religion Fast Facts." *DidYouKnow*. DidYouKnow, 2009. Web. 04 July 2012.

"Religious Groups' Official Positions on Stem Cell Research." *The Accidental Advocate*. Accidental Advocate, 2009. Web. 31 July 2012.

"Thirty Years' War." *eNotes*. eNotes. 2012. Web. 1 Aug. 2012.

"Top Ten Organized Religions of the World." *InfoPlease*. Pearson Education, 2012. Web. 31 July 2012.

Persuasive Essay #2

Morals in Modern Life

For hundreds of years, Religion was considered the definer of morality in a society and a model for the laws of society. With the flow of history governments have adopted policies to rid their laws and governing bodies of religion, but whether religion dictates morality has remained a heated and ongoing debate. In our modern world we are aware of and live with many varying religions and systems of belief, but would the absence of those mean the end of our morality? Does a moral compass exist without the existence of a deity? Would our society still function without religion? Does the belief in a system of religion or in a god inherently make one moral? Though many argue for religions as the basis of morality, scientists, philosophers and ordinary people have observed in modern time that both on a personal level and in society morality is not exclusively connected to religion.

The English philosopher Bernard Williams states, "Either one's motives for following the moral word of God are moral motives, or they are not. If they are, then one is already equipped with moral motivations, and the introduction of God adds nothing extra ... we reach the conclusion that any appeal to God in this connection adds to nothing at all" (Williams). Williams suggests that before the introduction of the idea of a god, people already possess a sense of morality. Williams says that moral people choose to follow a moral religion, and not that religion makes one moral. If this is the case, do we need religion? Why has it come to dominate the hearts and minds of millions of people? Does it serve a purpose?

"Religions certainly do provide a framework within which people can learn the difference between right and wrong" (Dixon). With this statement Thomas Dixon provides the function of religion in morality. However this also implies that religion is a system for conveying morals as schools are systems for conveying knowledge. Just as the schools themselves do not invent or discover the knowledge they impart to students, neither did religions invent the moral compass. It is in fact backwards to suggest that morality comes out of religion. Continuing with the school analogy, just as a school doesn't exist without something to teach, a religion doesn't exist without moral ideas to dispense.

Where then do our morals come from? Some scientists and social philosophers believe that we evolved morals in order to survive as group animals. Because we live in a social environment, we had to learn to curb our behaviors to suit group life. Basically this is the scientific equivalent of the 'Golden Rule.' Rousseau, in his social contract, outlines how we all sacrifice absolute freedom to protect ourselves from those who would do us harm, and in return we do not do harm to others. By willingly restricting our own behavior based on the rules of society, we have an expectation that others will do the same and therefore we are protected from certain transgressions by society. This implies that simple self-preservation is the basis for morality.

Can a person, then, be moral if she don't subscribe to a religion? Is religion the only way that people learn the moral tenants of our culture? Certainly not. There are many structures built into modern life that teach us how to behave in society. The family unit is the most important part of developing a sense of morality. Schools educate children from early ages how to survive and contribute in a social setting. All of society is set up in a way so that individuals function to serve the greater good. This is done through socialization, or the imparting of morality.

Though it appears clear that morals do not come from religion and a person without religious beliefs can be moral, are religious people more moral than those who don't believe in anything? The answer, surprisingly, is no. Social Psychological and Personality Science journal conducted a test in which non-religious people had higher scores showing that they were more inclined to show generosity and random acts of kindness, such as lending their possessions or offering a seat on a crowded bus or train. Religious people also had lower scores when it came to being charitable in other ways, including showing compassion to non-believers (Anwar 5).

Appendix: Student Essays

It is clear from this study that people without religion are more generous, which could only benefit society. It can only be hypothesized as to why non-religious people are more giving; I am of the opinion that religion creates barriers between people causing them to feel alienation or separation from those outside of their group, the 'us versus them' phenomenon. Phil Zuckerman's 2008 book, *Society Without God*, notes that Denmark and Sweden, "which are probably the least religious countries in the world, and possibly in the history of the world", enjoy "among the lowest violent crime rates in the world [and] the lowest levels of corruption in the world" (Zuckerman). An interesting fact to note about our country is that nearly "75 percent of Americans are God-fearing Christians; 75 percent of prisoners are God-fearing Christians. 10 percent of Americans are atheists; 0.2 percent of prisoners are atheists" (Gervais).

Some even argue that the teachings of some religions are specifically amoral. The teachings of Judaism and Christianity depict scenes of slavery and murder that are totally sanctioned by God. Hinduism has no strong ban on murder, saying that there are situations when taking another's life is acceptable (Menski 5). All of these things are frowned upon by our modern morals and are often overlooked or justified by leaders or practitioners of these religions by explaining some historical context. Of course morality changes based on the period in history and the society, but religions are supposed to be eternal and without error, because they are the expressions of a divine and perfect god. Despite the fact that religions are often strange relics of a specific and long past time, many people choose to take their morals from one of these institutions and ignore any uncomfortable truths.

Though religions teach morality, they are not the source of them. The scientific reasons for morality are seeded in the basis of society and are the only reason that it is able to work. We need morals to make us good people. All people have a sense of morality, but that doesn't imply that all people subscribe to a religious belief or that belief in a god is required to gain morality.

Works Cited

Anwar, Yasmin. "Highly Religious People Are Less Motivated by Compassion Than Are Non-Believers." *Science Daily*. 30 April 2012: 5. Print.

Dixon, Thomas. *Science and Religion: A Very Short Introduction*. Oxford: Oxford University Press, 2008.

Gervais, Ricky. "Why I'm an Atheist." Arts & Entertainment. *The Wall Street Journal*. 19 December 2010. Web. 1 Aug. 2012. <http://blogs.wsj.com/speak easy/2010/12/19/a-holiday-message-from-ricky-gervais-why-im-an-ath eist/>.

Menski, Werner. "Hinduism." Ethical Issues in Six Religious Traditions. Comp. Peggy Morgan. Second Ed. New York: Columbia University Press, 2007.

Rousseau, Jean-Jacques. "The Social Contract." *Book I*. 1. 1762. Print.

Williams, Bernard. *Morality*. Cambridge: Cambridge University Press, 1972.

Zuckerman, Phil. *Society Without God: What the Least Religious Nations Can Tell Us about Contentment*. New York: New York University Press, 2008.

Response Essay Assignment

For this assignment, students were to respond to one or more of the stories/essays that we read during that particular part of the course. They had to have a main idea, or a thesis statement, that their response was centered around. Their essay could take the form of a letter to the author or it could be a more "objective" critique/response written to a general audience. Students might connect their chosen story or essay to current events or contemporary examples of the issue at hand (for instance, immigration, the public role of religion, race, gender, or class issues, etc.). They could draw on their own experiences in the world to support their response. A simple summary would not suffice. Students could briefly summarize the main ideas, point to or quote particular passages, etc., but they needed to take a position in responding to the story/essay and support that position with their own critical thinking and examples. They were not required to write about religion.

Response Essay

The Bible's Influence on the
Founding of the United States

Throughout history, literature has had a profound influence on laws and legal trends. One only has to remember the impact that "Uncle

Tom's Cabin" by Harriet Beecher Stowe had first on the abolitionist movement, then on the general population in the north, and eventually the political structure of the nation as a whole. One could also cite Harper Lee's "To Kill a Mockingbird" and its effect on the civil rights movement or Upton Sinclair's "The Jungle" and its influence on federal regulations on meat processing and packaging. While all of these pieces of literature were important and positive inspirations on movements that led to changes in law, there is one piece of literature that had a profound influence on our most basic ideas about law and how we govern ourselves. While the founding fathers were influenced by many sources when establishing our republic, it will be shown that some of the founders' most basic and innate beliefs about the law are derived from the ethics, laws and moral suppositions laid down in the Bible. This includes the equality of all men under the law, and the need for systems such as the Rule of Law and checks and balances because of the sinful nature of man.

In order to adequately support the profound relationship between the Bible and the founding of our country, it must be shown that the crafters of our nation had a deep belief in and connection to the Bible. While it is obvious that not all the founders were practicing Christians, they accepted the philosophical tenets of the faith. While it is inaccurate to describe the United States as a Christian nation, it has to be understood that its founding principles were seen by its first citizens through a Christian lens. This is because both the founders and the early citizens shared the Christian worldview. As John Adams stated in 1798, "Our Constitution was made only for a moral and religious people. It is wholly inadequate to the government of any other." The founders believed that the backbone of a free society was strong religious people in their private lives. George Washington said, "Religion and morality are the essential pillars of civil society." The Continental Congress issued the following statement in 1778: "Whereas true religion and good morals are the only solid foundations of public liberty and happiness...." In addition, John Adams said in 1776 that "It is religion and morality alone which can establish the principles upon which freedom can securely stand." The founders clearly thought that religion was indispensable in a free and democratic society.

The fundamental principle that the founding fathers used in establishing the new government of the United States was the idea that all men are equal before the law. When Thomas Jefferson wrote in The Declaration of Independence that "all men are created equal," where did he get this idea? Most cultures throughout history, and even some today, reject this proposition. Indeed, it seems absurd to claim that all men are equal when it is quite obvious to anyone that men are unequal in size, physical strength, intellect, integrity and just about every other way. Jefferson felt strongly, however, that all men are equal; he states "We hold these truths to be self-evident." The equality that Jefferson was referring to is the fact that all men are moral equals. They do not behave equally well, but their lives have a moral worth no greater or less than anyone else. The worth of an ordinary laborer was no less than that of Jefferson himself. The concept that every life has equal value was at the time a uniquely Christian idea. The Bible states that every human life is of infinite value to God and that he loves everyone equally. Galatians 3–28 states that "There is neither Jew nor Greek, there is neither slave nor free, there is no male and female, for you are all one in Christ Jesus. And if you are Christ's, then you are Abraham's offspring, heirs according to promise." The recognition by law of the intrinsic value of each human being did not exist in ancient times. Among the Romans, law protected social institutions such as the patriarchal family but it did not safeguard the basic rights of the individual. Christianity changed all of that. It introduced the idea that the rights of the individual took precedence over the rights of social institutions.

When Jefferson says that this fact is self-evident he means that it is self-evident because it is in agreement with the laws of nature. The idea of an innate natural law is a biblical concept. Romans 13:5 talks about the fact that human beings intuitively know what is right because God has given them a conscience. The concept of a natural moral law was accepted by not only Jefferson. Kermit L. Hall notes in his book, *The Oxford Guide to Supreme Court Decisions,* that the first few Chief Justices to the Supreme Court argued publicly that the Court could strike down an act of Congress if it violated natural law (498–99). John Hancock, the first signer of the Declaration of Independence, asserted that when the laws of man are in conflict with the laws of nature and impose on our God-given rights, our duty is clear. He states, "Resistance to tyranny becomes the Christian and social duty of each individual.... Continue steadfast and, with a proper sense of your dependence on God, nobly defend those rights which heaven gave, and no man ought to take from us." Samuel Adams suggested that man's law should hold in relation to the law of nature when he stated, "Just and true liberty, equal and impartial liberty, in matters spiritual and temporal, is a thing that all men are clearly entitled to by the eternal and immutable laws of God and nature, as well as by the law of nations and all well-grounded municipal laws, which must have their foundation in the former."

Besides the belief in the dignity and moral equality of every human being, the founding fathers' faith also taught them that humans were sinful. The doctrine that all men are in a fallen and sinful state can be found in Romans 5:12; "Wherefore, as by one man sin entered the world, and death by sin; and so death passed onto all men, for that all have sinned." As James Madison wrote in Federalist No. 51, "If men were angels, no government would be necessary." Not only did the founding fathers recognize that government was necessary to prevent unscrupulous individuals from taking advantage of others, they came up with a brilliant system of checks and balances to insure that no individual governmental body or person could obtain enough power to sacrifice the well being of the people for their own self interest. The establishment of the Rule of Law and the system of checks and balances are bold affirmations of the founders' belief in the Biblical principle that human beings are members of a fallen and sinful race. The founding fathers' realistic view of the sinful nature of man prevented them from falling into the trap of attempting to replace one oppressive ruler with another ruler who they would have hoped would be more benevolent.

While it is accurate to say that the founders of this nation drew from many influences when constructing the laws and precepts that govern our society, it is undeniable that they depended on the principles found in the Bible to a large degree. These principles were so ingrained in them that they assumed them without debate. The uniquely Christian concept of the equality of all men formed the basis for every aspect of the Constitution. The assumption that no man deserves absolute power over his fellow countrymen due to his fallen and sinful nature led to the idea for the separation of powers and the doctrine of checks and balances. When the founders wrote the Constitution using these basic biblical concepts, they had the luxury of knowing that their fellow countrymen shared these same tenets because the Christian philosophy was taken for granted as being inherently true. To restate George Washington's quote, "Religion and morality are the essential pillars of civil society." In conclusion, if not for the influence of the Bible on the founding fathers the laws that govern this country would surely be very different.

Works Cited

Adams, John. "John Adams." BrainyQuote.com. Xplore. 2013. 12 September 2013.

New York State. *Public Papers of Governor, Volume 4*. Albany: James B. Lyon, 1900. Print.

Washington, George. "George Washington." ringthebellsoffreedom.com. 12 September 2013.

Hancock, John. "John Hancock." *christianity.about.com*. About.com. 12 September 2013.

Adams, Samuel. "Samuel Adams." *press-pubs.uchicago.edu*. University of Chicago, 1987. 12 September 2013.

Hall, Kermit. *The Oxford Guide to Supreme Court Decisions*. New York: Oxford University Press, 2005. Print.

Personal Narrative Assignment

For this assignment students were to write a personal narrative; that is, tell a story. They could choose the topic—maybe something that happened to them, or something they heard from someone or somewhere else. It could push the boundaries of fiction—they were encouraged to use their imagination and be creative. They needed an introduction, several body paragraphs, and a conclusion. Students were asked to write in the first person, and to think about telling their story in chronological order. The story had to make sense and have a central point.

Personal Narrative #1

Religion in My Life

Religion is a subject that was discussed throughout our book and it seems to be a topic of much discussion in this country and across the world. There are thousands of religions and they have been discussed and debated since the beginning of time and it seems the discussion will never end. Our founding fathers discussed this topic and had the foresight to write about it. Our Constitution states, "Congress shall make no law respecting an establishment of religion, or prohibiting the free exercise thereof." Of course this does not seem to stop elected officials, people, or organizations from putting forth their own agenda. Religion can be difficult to define because everyone seems to have a different idea, opinion, or definition of exactly what religion is and how it should be used. Religion should not be forced upon anyone. There are many beliefs, values, and morals that differ among individuals so it is difficult to standardize or compartmentalize religion and what is right or wrong. Religion can be a very divisive and conflict-ridden subject for some individuals and there seems to be multiple sides as to why we need or even want religion.

I believe religion is in the eye of the beholder. I have had many personal experiences with religion and my perspective has swayed from time to time as I have learned to take a broader view. I grew up in a house where I experienced a change from having no religion to an environment that was extremely religious and it happened almost overnight. My parents were looking to change the way they were living life and turned to God and became Christians. Christians have been praised and ridiculed for many years for how they approach their religion. There are extremists in every religion; however, I would argue that Christians are ridiculed more than any other religion in this country. There are thousands of points of view on how religion should or should not be communicated and shared. I believe that those who judge individuals who follow their beliefs walk a very thin line.

I was 13 when my parents made the decision to follow God and this was a very difficult time for my siblings and me. We felt like we were being indoctrinated. Our lives were turned upside down. We were forced to follow their path and it is something that to this day causes intense discussions. Of course children have been forced to go to church for many years. In "The Man That Loved Children" Jo believed that if "they are forced to go to School, then they should be forced to go to Church," (Stead 109). Several activities that we had taken for granted were no longer a viable option. We could no longer watch television or go to the movies. They literally removed all the televisions from our house. Of course this was in the mid 1980's so that did not take very much time. Listening to music was deterred unless it was Christian related.

We were required to attend church three days a week. I will never forget the first time I attended this event. Once we found ourselves a place to sit everyone started to sing. After the first few songs my family was asked to stand up and be recognized and everyone applauded. I thought I just scored the winning basket in a basketball game. The very first intermission everyone started coming up to us and thanking us and asking us questions. They asked if this was the first time we had ever attended church and repeatedly told us how much we will fit in. I felt exactly like Cecilia did in Donald Barthelme's "A City of Churches" (503).

On Sundays we would leave early in the morning and would not return home until the late evening and for a fan of a professional football team (Steelers) this made it even harder to deal with. When I reflect on this point in my life I realize that this was the point in time where my foundation and my initial ideology on religion were built. As a young individual one could only imagine that this would cause me to have a disdain or hatred for religion forever. One would surmise that I had many rebellious altercations with my parents on how they should be raising me. I tried to have many conversations on what this "religious" experience was doing to me and of course that always fell on deaf ears. I would always get the "as long as you live under my roof" speech that I am sure most children receive when they do not agree with their parents. As they say, I grinned and bared it until I graduated High School. I moved out the weekend after I graduated and never attended church on a regular basis again. Oh, and I bought a TV stat! Weddings, Christmas, Easter, and funerals are my only exceptions; however, the door is always open as my Mother and Father repeatedly tell me. With that said, my perspective on religion has changed as I have grown older and I have passed on my religious knowledge or acumen, if you will, on to my children in a much different fashion than I received it.

Whenever my children ask about religion or even church as they frequently do because many of their friends attend, I give them as much information as possible. I even purchased them a picture Bible so they can read about the stories that they hear about. A few years ago my oldest son was struck by the curiosity bug and wanted to attend a service and I paved the way for him to go. Of course he went with my mother. I did give her strict marching orders and my wife went along for the ride. Neither of my sons bring the subject up of attending church anymore, however we do discuss religion and the fact that people should not be persecuted for believing what they want to believe in.

I am often asked about my stance on religion and God and I always try to stay unbiased and express to them that I am neutral on the topic. More specifically, I am asked if I believe in God and my response is always, yes, I do. I believe in a higher power and I also believe we can all believe what we want when religion is the topic. In spite of my experiences I carry no ill will toward religion or those that decide to live without religion. With that said, I do have a strong opinion on the subject, which is that it should never involve any force from anyone. I also believe that it is not necessary for an individual to attend church three or even seven days a week to show that they believe in God or to be considered religious. Of course I am sure there are many out there that may disagree with that sentiment.

Some people still feel obligated to be a member of some religious group in order to live in their society. There are those that favor religion when it benefits them and then ignore it when it does not fit in their predicament. I have always been of the opinion that attending church or believing in the church is a personal decision. Personal decisions can change and they can be swayed by television, radio, and the Internet.

There are always headlines in the news or on the Internet that reference religious activities. Some of these stories show or portray the good qualities of religion, however there are many examples of where it is quite the opposite. With the 24-hour cable news cycle and the information highway (also known as the Internet) we can read, listen, or even watch whatever religious sermon we choose. Even if someone has never heard of a specific religion they can just Google religion and literally millions of pages will be instantly available for research. The information on any religion is at our fingertips, however individuals must be careful with which sites they acquire their information from. Just like writing a report, citing sources is extremely important. When it comes to my own research on religions, or whenever I am reading an article, I always take the source into consideration.

An article I recently read from ABC news about the Westboro Baptist Church out of Topeka, Kansas discusses an entire new level that certain religious organizations have gone too while hiding behind a religious shield (Jones 2012). This group travels to military funerals and pickets them along with desecrating on the American flag and other improper acts. As a member of the military this controversial church and their actions are very difficult to comprehend. This church gives all Baptist churches a bad name. Even though the average person can understand that this is not the normal techniques, tactics, or procedures that a church complies with, it is very disingenuous to come from a church.

I try to look at the positives in all stories and through further research they can be found. This organization has brought so much attention upon them that ordinary citizens have bonded around these events and protested them. These groups stand between Westboro protesters and the families of the fallen so the grieving families cannot hear or see them. Regardless of background, denomination, social class, or political leaning people show up to support the families of the fallen.

In closing, I must say that I have come to appreciate the view I received as a young teenager attending church. For me, the first-hand experience was necessary so I could be better informed to understand religion and pass that on to my children and respect the positions of others on the subject. Regardless of how I was introduced into religion and the church I quickly adapted to what my parents expected me to do and I have lived to talk about it. Does this mean I agree with them forcing religion down my throat? No. Would I do that? No. Would I expect someone else to do that? No! This is a divisive topic that will continue to stir debates among families, friends, and others all over the world.

Works Cited

Barthelme, Donald. "A City of Churches." *The Best American Short Stories of the Century.* Boston: Houghton Mifflin, 1999.

Jones, D. "Westboro Church Protesters Confronted by Zombies." *ABC News.* 30 July 2012. <http://abcnews.go.com/blogs/headlines/2012/07/westboro-church-protesters-confronted-by-zombies/>.

Stead, C. *The Man That Loved Children.* Victoria, Australia: Melbourne University. 2 Aug 2012. <http://books.google.com/books?id=vQDtgxtFpIkC&printsec=frontcover&dq=The+Man+that+Loved+Children&source=bl&ots=HESJ8JhU7D&sig=5OwMtXHyWfmkzOGyrJecWbucrkM&hl=en&sa=X&ei=100cUKaRG4W4rQGf6YHwCg&ved=0CC4Q6AEwAA#v=

onepage&q=The percent20Man percent20that percent20Loved percent20Children&f=false>.

Personal Narrative #2

Finding God: My Life Story

My name is [John S.] and this is a short story of my life. I was born and raised in Ohio. My parents who adopted me are [Dave and Betty S.]; they have always cared for me and have watched me grow up for the last twenty-five years. I also have six siblings: three brothers and three sisters. My mom and dad raised me in a Christian home and we were a part of the local church called, *Freedom Christian Fellowship,* or *FCF* for short. It was a family oriented Church that we were very active in. You would think that by me being raised in a Christian home and going to church that I would be a good kid. But, I had to learn life the hard way and take my own road.

I went to Milan school district and had a lot of problems; being the only black kid in my grade caused problems for me. I got into fights every day. I was picked on, beat up, and I hated going to school. My mom pulled me out in 3rd grade and home-schooled me. I went to kid's church and loved all of it; I made friends there and learned about God. I learned that God created the world, the universe, and everything in existence. We were taught that when we died we would go to heaven if we had Jesus in our hearts. However, if we didn't, we would go to hell. This is a true fact, but I did not understand it fully. All I did was say the prayer they told me to pray, hoping that it alone would save me. I went on with my life not knowing that the prayer I prayed wouldn't save me from going to hell.

I went into middle school making friends, memories, and learning music. I played drums, played on the worship team, and played in the youth band. I also started my own band called *Oreo,* whose members included my brother Alex, my friend Steve, and myself. I had a lot of good times in youth group and church. They took up most of my life; we were having so much fun together.

High school came and I started hanging out with my brother and his friends more often. I couldn't drive so I went with my brother a lot to have some fun. Everything he did, I did; slowly I started to push all limits. Girls started to become more desirable; I started dating more and became very promiscuous. I started smoking, drinking, partying, and started handling drugs as well. There were a few times I went to church hung over and played drums on my worship team. Life was starting to get bad; I wanted to find pleasure and acceptance anywhere I could find it. I started to play in bigger bands and began to attract more attention. I wanted to be noticed; I wanted to be seen; I wanted acceptance; I wanted love; but after everything I did, nothing was enough.

I met my future wife at a festival in Port Clinton, and a few years after that we were married. She was 18 and I was 20; we were in love (or so we thought). Getting married young caused us a lot of problems and we learned life together the hard way. We fought a lot, and married life wasn't what I thought it was going to be. I wanted to be happy, yet everywhere I went, I never found true happiness. Something always seemed to be missing.

I was driving on State Rte. 250 one day when God spoke to me, telling me to turn around and go back to the church I just passed. So I did! I went in and they were having youth group. I met the youth pastor (Ryan Lane), and over time we became very good friends. We started hanging out a lot and he started to show me things about God that I never knew. He gave me books and audio sermons to listen to, and slowly I started to see that I was not a Christian by the life I was living. I knew everything about church and religion, but I knew nothing about God and His Son Jesus Christ.

I ended up meeting a guy named Mike Reynolds from a band called ForToday. We started talking while he showed me verses from the Bible that I never knew about which condemned my heart. More and more I started to see that I wasn't a Christian according to the Bible; now I had proof from the Bible that I wasn't right with God. I went through a period of time questioning what I knew, because now I knew nothing. So on a car ride home God showed me how far away from Him I really was; I wanted to be close to Him. He made me; He is the only one that could take away all the pain, addictions, and suicidal tendencies.

I gave my life to Christ on October 9th 2012. Now I want to know everything I can about Jesus and His plan for my life. I still have problems in life (we all do), but now I have my creator in my life to guide me through everything. I don't have any more addictions; I don't fight or party or drink or smoke. All of my suicidal tendencies are gone, and I love my life. Jesus has saved me from death and brought me back to life again. My sin separated me from God, but through the death of Jesus on the cross, I can now be connected to God and know who He truly is:

> For the wrath of God is revealed from heaven against all ungod-liness and unrighteousness of men who suppress the truth in unrighteousness, because that which is known about God is evident within them; for God made it evident to them. For since the creation of the world His invisible attributes, His eternal power and divine nature, have been clearly seen, being understood through what has been made, so that they are without excuse.—Romans 1:18–20

> Jesus answered, "Truly, truly, I say to you, unless one is born of water and the Spirit he cannot enter into the kingdom of God. That which is born of the flesh is flesh, and that which is born of the Spirit is spirit.—John 3:5–6

> Or do you not know that the unrighteous will not inherit the kingdom of God? Do not be deceived; neither fornicators, nor idolaters, nor adulterers, nor effeminate, nor homosexuals, nor thieves, nor the covetous, nor drunkards, nor revilers, nor swindlers, will inherit the kingdom of God.—1 Corinthians 6:9–10

> For who among men knows the thoughts of a man except the spirit of the man which is in him? Even so the thoughts of God no one knows except the Spirit of God. Now we have received, not the spirit of the world, but the Spirit who is from God, so that we may know the things freely given to us by God, which things we also speak, not in words taught by human wisdom, but in those taught by the Spirit, combining spiritual thoughts with spiritual words.
>
> But a natural man does not accept the things of the Spirit of God, for they are foolishness to him; and he cannot understand them, because they are spiritually appraised.—1 Corinthians 2:11–14

> Everyone who practices sin also practices lawlessness; and sin is lawlessness. You know that He appeared in order to take away sins; and in Him there is no sin. No one who abides in Him sins; no one who sins has seen Him or knows Him. Little children, make sure no one deceives you; the one who practices righteousness is righteous, just as He is righteous; the one who

practices sin is of the devil; for the devil has sinned from the beginning. The Son of God appeared for this purpose, to destroy the works of the devil. No one who is born of God practices sin, because His seed abides in him; and he cannot sin, because he is born of God. By this the children of God and the children of the devil are obvious: Anyone who does not practice righteousness is not of God, nor the one who does not love his brother.—1st John 3:4–10

Works Cited

Agee, James. *A Death in the Family*. New York: Avon, 1965.

Bakewell, Sarah. *How to Live: Or a Life of Montaigne in One Question and Twenty Attempts at an Answer*. New York: Other Press, 2010.

Barnet, Sylvan. *A Short Guide to Writing about Art*. New York: Pearson, 2005.

Barth, Karl. *The Word of God and the Word of Man*. Trans. Douglas Horton. New York: Harper and Row, 1957.

Beecher, Henry Ward. *Lectures and Orations by Henry Ward Beecher*. Ed. Newell Dwight Hillis. New York: Fleming H. Revell, 1913.

_____, and Edna Dean Proctor. *Life Thoughts Gathered from the Extemporaneous Discourses of Henry Ward Beecher*. Boston: Phillips, Sampson and Co., 1858.

Bernstein, Nina. "Clinton Cites Bible to Attack Immigration Bill." *New York Times* 15 April 2006: A19.

Berthoff, Ann. *The Making of Meaning*. Montclair: Boynton Cook, 1981.

Bhabha, Homi. *The Location of Culture*. New York: Routledge, 1994.

Biema, David Van. "Rebels in the Pews." *Time* 17 Jun 2002: 54–64.

Biliczky, Carol. "Taxpayers Fund Religion: College Teaches 'Biblical Truth' to Public High School Students." *Beacon Journal* 9 Feb 2014: A1.

Bizzell, Patricia. "Beyond Anti-Foundationalism to Rhetorical Authority: Problems Defining 'Cultural Literacy.'" *College English* 52 (1990): 661–75.

_____, and Bruce Herzberg. *Negotiating Difference: Cultural Case Studies for Composition*. Boston: Bedford Books, 1996.

Bloom, Harold. *How to Read and Why*. New York: Touchstone, 2000.

Boswell, Marshall. "Updike, Religion, and the Novel of Moral Debate." *The Cambridge Companion to John Updike*. Ed. Stacey Olster. Cambridge: Cambridge University Press, 2006.

Cain, Jeffrey P. "(Sacra) Mentality: Catholic Identity in the Postmodern Classroom." *Negotiating Religious Faith in the Composition Classroom*. Eds. Elizabeth Vander Lei and bonnie lenore kyburz. Portsmouth: Boynton/Cook, 2005. 167–83.

Carson, Rachel. "The Marginal World." *The Best American Essays of the*

Century. Ed. Joyce Carol Oates. New York: Houghton Mifflin, 2001. 214–19.

Carter, Stephen L. *The Culture of Disbelief*. New York: Anchor Books, 1993.

Cervantes, Miguel de. *The Portable Cervantes*. New York: The Viking Press, 1966.

Chafets, Zev. "Ministers of Debate." *The New York Times Magazine*. 19 March 2006: 55+.

Chandler, Daniel Ross. "Henry Ward Beecher: A Nation's Tribune." Gettysburg Conf. on Rhetorical Transactions in the Civil War Era. Gettysburg. 25 Jun 1983.

Chekhov, Anton. *The Image of Chekhov*. Trans. Robert Payne. New York: Knopf, 1963.

Chua-Eoan, Howard. "Second Act: How Benedict XVI May Become More Influential After His Resignation." *Time*. 25 Feb 2013: 19–23.

Contact. Dir. Robert Zemeckis. Perf. Jodi Foster, Matthew McConaughey, Angela Bassett, John Hurt. Warner Bros., 1997. Film.

Critchlow, Donald T. *Phyllis Schlafly and Grassroots Conservatism: A Woman's Crusade*. Princeton: Princeton University Press, 2005.

Daniell, Beth. *A Communion of Friendship: Literacy, Spiritual Practice, and Women in Recovery*. Carbondale: Southern Illinois University Press, 2003.

Dawkins, Madalyn. "Dodging the God Squad." *The Chronicle of Higher Education*. 26 Aug 2013. 28 Aug 2013. <http://chronicle.com/article/Dodging-the-God-Squad/121247/?cid=oh&utm>.

Dawkins, Richard, and Jerry Coyne. "One Side Can Be Wrong." *The Seagull Reader: Essays*. 2nd ed. Ed. Joseph Kelly. New York: W. W. Norton, 2008. 69–74.

Deans, Thomas. "The Rhetoric of Jesus Writing in the Story of the Woman Accused of Adultery (John 7.53–8.11)." *College Composition and Communication* 65.3 (2014): 406–29.

Delbanco, Andrew. *College: What it Was, Is, and Should Be*. Princeton: Princeton University Press, 2012.

DePalma, Michael-John. "Re-envisioning Religious Discourses as Rhetorical Resources in Composition Teaching: A Pragmatic Response to the Challenge of Belief." *College Composition and Communication* 63.2 (2011): 219–43.

DeStigter, Todd. "Baseball, Apple Pie, and God: Inquiring about Religion in American Public Life." *English Education* 37.1 (Oct 2004): 75–79.

Dewey, John. *A Common Faith*. New Haven: Yale University Press, 1934.

———. *Democracy and Education*. New York: Macmillan, 1916.

———. "The Need for a Recovery of Philosophy." *On Experience, Nature, and Freedom: Representative Selections*. New York: Bobbs-Merrill, 1960. 19–69.

_____. *The Philosophy of John Dewey*. Ed. John J. McDermott. Chicago: University of Chicago Press, 1973.

_____. *Quest for Certainty*. New York: Capricorn, 1929.

_____. "Ralph Waldo Emerson." *Characters and Events*. New York: Holt, Rinehart, and Winston, 1929. 1:73, 74.

Douglass, Frederick. *Narrative of the Life of Frederick Douglass, an American Slave*. Boston: Anti-Slavery Office, 1845.

Douthat, Ross. "The Future of the Santorum Coalition." *New York Times*. 7 March 2012. <http://campaignstops.blogs.nytimes.com/2012/03/07/the-future-of-the-santorum-coalition/?_php=true&_type=blogs&_r=0>.

Dowd, Michael. *Thank God for Evolution: How the Marriage of Science and Religion Will Transform Your Life and Our World*. New York: Viking, 2007.

Edmundson, Mark. *Why Read?* New York: Bloomsbury, 2004.

Egan, Timothy. "Theocracy and Its Discontents." *The New York Times*. 23 Feb 2012. 23 Feb 2012. <http://opinionator.blogs.nytimes.com/2012/02/23/theocracy-and-its-discontents/?>.

Elbow, Peter, and Pat Belanoff. *Sharing and Responding*. New York: Random House, 1989.

Emerson, Ralph Waldo. *The Portable Emerson*. Ed. Carl Bode. New York: Penguin Books, 1946.

Family Research Council. Home Page. 2 April 2007. <http://www.frc.org/about-frc>.

Feldman, Noah. *Divided by God: America's Church-State Problem—And What We Should Do about It*. New York: Farrar, Straus, & Giroux, 2005.

Fernandez-Armesto, Felipe. *Truth: A History and a Guide for the Perplexed*. New York: Thomas Dunne Books, 1997.

Fish, Stanley. "One University Under God?" *Chronicle of Higher Education*. 7 Jan 2005. 12 Feb 2007. <http://chronicle.com/jobs/2005/01/2005010701c.html>.

_____. "Rick Santorum Isn't Crazy." *New York Times*. 5 Mar 2012. <http://opinionator.blogs.nytimes.com/2012/03/05/rick-santorum-isnt-crazy/>.

_____. *Save the World on Your Own Time*. Oxford: Oxford University Press, 2008.

_____. "What Should Colleges Teach?" *New York Times*. Opinionator. 31 Aug 2009. <http://opinionator.blogs.nytimes.com/2009/09/07/what-should-colleges-teach-part-3/?_php=true&_type=blogs&_r=0>.

Fitzgerald, F. Scott. "The Crack-Up." *The Best American Essays of the Century*. Ed. Joyce Carol Oates. New York: Houghton Mifflin, 2001. 139–52.

Flower, Elizabeth, and Murray Murphey. *A History of Philosophy in America*. Vol. 2. New York: G. P. Putnam, 1977.

Freedman, Samuel G. "In Gospel Songs of Yore, Clues to the Speeches of

Martin Luther King, Jr." *New York Times.* 14 Jun 2013. 26 Jun 2013. <http://www.nytimes.com/2013/06/15/us/martin-luther-king-jr-sermons.html?emc=etal>.

Freedom from Religion Foundation. *New York Times.* 23 Jun 2013: 2 Sunday Review.

Freire, Paulo. *Pedagogy of the Oppressed.* Trans. Myra Bergman Ramos. New York: Continuum, 1999.

Gass, Susan M., and Larry Selinker. *Second Language Acquisition: An Introductory Course.* New York: Routledge, 2008.

Gilyard, Keith. *Let's Flip the Script.* Detroit: Wayne State, 1996.

Gould, Stephen Jay. *Rocks of Ages: Science and Religion in the Fullness of Life.* New York: Ballantine Books, 1999.

Hairston, Maxine. "Diversity, Ideology, and Teaching Writing." *Cross Talk in Comp Theory: A Reader.* Ed. Victor Villanueva. Urbana, Ill.: NCTE, 1997. 659–75.

Harris, Sam. *The End of Faith: Religion, Terror, and the Future of Reason.* New York: W.W. Norton, 2004.

_____. "The Myth of 'Moderation' in Religion." *The Seagull Reader: Essays.* 2nd ed. Ed. Joseph Kelly. New York: W. W. Norton, 2008. 123–28.

Hosanna-Tabor Evangelical Lutheran Church and School v. EEOC. 565 U.S. (2012).

Howard, Gerald. "The View from Bay Ridge, 1960." *New York Times.* 5 March 2012. <http://campaignstops.blogs.nytimes.com/2012/03/05/the-view-from-bay-ridge-in-1960/>.

Howard, John R. *Henry Ward Beecher: A Study of His Personality, Career, and Influence in Public Affairs.* New York: Fords, Howard, and Hulbert, 1891.

Hylton, Wil S. "Lights, Action: The Alternate Realities of James Turrell." *The New York Times Magazine.* 16 Jun 2013: 34.

Jablonski, Carol J. "Rhetoric, Paradox, and the Movement for Women's Ordination in the Roman Catholic Church." *Quarterly Journal of Speech* 74.2 (May 1988): 164–83.

Jacoby, Susan. "A New Birth of Reason." *The American Scholar.* Winter 2013: 20–31.

James, William. *A Pluralistic Universe.* Cambridge: Harvard University Press, 1977.

_____. *Pragmatism.* Amherst: Prometheus Books, 1991.

_____. *Talks to Teachers on Psychology; and to Students on Some of Life's Ideals.* New York: W.W. Norton, 1958.

_____. *The Varieties of Religious Experience.* New York: Barnes and Noble Classics, 2004.

_____. "The Will to Believe." *Essays in Pragmatism*. New York: Hafner, 1948.

Kaman, Al. "George W. Bush and the G-Word." *Washington Post*. 14 Oct 2005. 20 Jan 2013. <www.washingtonpost.com/wp-dyn/content/article/2005/10/13/AR2005101301688.html>.

Kaplan, Esther. *With God on their Side*. New York: The New Press, 2004.

Kennedy, John F. *Transcript: Address to Greater Houston Ministerial Association*. 12 Sep 1960. 9 Jan 2014. <http://www.npr.org/templates/story/story.php?storyId=16920600>.

Kluger, Jeffrey. "The Biology of Belief." *TIME: Your Brain: A User's Guide*. New York: Time Home Entertainment, 2011.

Kornblut, Anne E. "Dean Makes Final Rounds as Party Chairman Race Ends." *New York Times*. 12 Jun 2006: A14.

Krashen, Stephen D. *Principles and Practice in Second Language Acquisition*. London: Prentice Hall International, 1981.

Kristof, Nicholas. "A Church Mary Can Love." *New York Times*. 18 April 2010:WK11 (New York edition).

Krugman, Paul. "John and Jerry." *New York Times*. 3 April 2006: A21.

Kushner, Tony. *Angels in America*. New York: Theatre Comm. Group, 1992.

Lambert, Frank. *Religion in American Politics: A Short History*. Princeton: Princeton University Press, 2008.

Langer, Susanne K. *Philosophy in a New Key: A Study in the Symbolism of Reason, Rite, and Art*. Cambridge: Harvard University Press, 1942.

Lei, Elizabeth Vander. "Coming to Terms with Religious Faith in the Composition Classroom: Introductory Comments." *Negotiating Religious Faith in the Composition Classroom*. Eds. Elizabeth Vander Lei and bonnie lenore kyburz. Portsmouth: Boynton/Cook, 2005.

Lewis, C. S. *Mere Christianity*. New York: Harper Collins, 2001.

_____. *Problem of Pain*. New York: Harper Collins, 2001.

Liell, Scott. "Shaking the Foundations of Faith." *New York Times*. 18 Nov 2005: A27.

Lira, Sonia. "Las estrategias de las parejas para resolver sus conflictos." *La Tercera*.25 July 2009: 6 Tendencias.

Lott, Bret. "Atonement." *The Seagull Reader: Essays*. 2nd ed. Ed. Joseph Kelly. New York: W. W. Norton, 2008. 217–19.

Macdonald, Loren B. *Life in the Making: An Approach to Religion through the Method of Modern Pragmatism*. Boston: Sherman, French & Co., 1911.

Mahony, Roger. "Called by God to Help." *New York Times* 22 March 2006: A29.

Malamud, Bernard. *The Fixer*. New York: Farrar, Straus, and Giroux, 1966.

McLoughlin, William G. *The Meaning of Henry Ward Beecher: An Essay on the Shifting Values of Mid-Victorian America, 1840–1870*. New York: Alfred A. Knopf, 1970.

Meacham, Jon. "A Papal Benediction." *Time*. 25 Feb 2013: 24.

Miles, Jack. *God: A Biography*. New York: Vintage, 1995.

Murray, Donald M. *The Craft of Revision*. 4th ed. Fort Worth: Harcourt, 2001.

Nocera, Joe. "A Revolutionary Idea." *The New York Times*. 02 Feb 2012. 02 Feb 2012. <http://www.nytimes.com/2012/02/25/opinion/nocera-a-revolutionary-idea.html?>.

Oates, Joyce Carol. "They All Just Went Away." *The Best American Essays of the Century*. Ed. Joyce Carol Oates. New York: Houghton Mifflin, 2001. 553–63.

Obama, Barack. "'Call to Renewal' Keynote Address." 28 Jun 2006. 12 July 2008. <http://www.obama.senate.gov/speech/060628-call_to_renewal/>.

_____. "Remarks by the President at the National Prayer Breakfast." 7 Feb 2013. 20 April 2013. <http://www.whitehouse.gov/the-press-office/2013/02/07/remarks-president-national-prayer-breakfast>.

O'Connor, Flannery. "Everything That Rises Must Converge." *Everything That Rises Must Converge*. New York: Farrar, Straus, and Giroux, 1970. 3–23.

Ostriker, Alicia Suskin. *Feminist Revision and the Bible*. Oxford: Blackwell, 1993.

Peirce, Charles S. *Charles Sanders Peirce: Selected Writings*. Ed. Philip P. Wiener. New York: Dover, 1958.

_____. *Collected Papers of Charles Sanders Peirce*. Eds. Charles Hartshorn and Paul Weiss. Vol. 8. Cambridge: Harvard University Press, 1931.

_____. "How to Make Our Ideas Clear." *Popular Science Monthly* 12 (Jan 1878): 286–302.

_____. *The Philosophy of Peirce: Selected Writings*. Ed. Justus Buchler. New York: Harcourt, 1940.

Perkins, Priscilla. "'A Radical Conversion of the Mind': Fundamentalism, Hermeneutics, and the Metanoic Classroom." *College English*. 63.5 (2001): 585–611.

Perry, Rick. Campaign Ad. 7 December 2011. 22 July 2013. <http://www.washingtonpost.com/blogs/the-fix/post/rick-perry-ad-condemns-obamas-war-on-religion/2011/12/07/gIQAZHpZcO_blog.html>.

Petrik, James. "In Defense of C. S. Lewis' Analysis of God's Goodness." *International Journal for Philosophy of Religion*. 36 (1994): 45–56.

Pirsig, Robert M. *Zen and the Art of Motorcycle Maintenance*. New York: HarperCollins, 2005.

Porter, Katherine Anne. "The Jilting of Granny Weatherall." *40 Short Stories: A Portable Anthology*. Ed. Beverly Lawn. Boston: Bedford/St. Martin's, 2009.

Ramsey, Bennett. *Submitting to Freedom: The Religious Vision of William James*. New York: Oxford University Press, 1993.

Rand, Lizabeth A. "Enacting Faith: Evangelical Discourse and the Discipline of Composition Studies." *College Composition and Communication* 52:3 (2001): 349–367.

ReligiousTolerence.org. "Falwell's Controversial Comments." 3 April 2007. <http://www.religioustolerence.org/falwell.htm>.

Ringer, Jeffrey M. "The Dogma of Inquiry: Composition and the Primacy of Faith." *Rhetoric Review* 32:3 (2013): 349–365.

Rorty, Richard. *Philosophy and Social Hope*. London: Penguin Books, 1999.

_____. *Rorty and His Critics*. Ed. Robert B. Brandom. Malden, MA: Blackwell, 2000.

_____, and Gianni Vattimo. *The Future of Religion*. Ed. Santiago Zabala. New York: Columbia University Press, 2005.

Roskelly, Hephzibah, and Kate Ronald. *Reason to Believe: Romanticism, Pragmatism, and the Teaching of Writing*. New York: State University of New York Press, 1998.

Saroyan, William. "Resurrection of a Life." *Best American Short Stories of the Century*. Ed. John Updike. Boston: Houghton Mifflin, 1999.

Scalia, Antonin. "God's Justice and Ours." *First Things* (May 2002): 17–21.

Shakespeare, William. *Hamlet. The Riverside Shakespeare*. 2nd ed. Eds. Herschel Baker, et. al. Boston: Houghton Mifflin, 1997.

Siker, Jeffrey S. "President Bush, Biblical Faith, and the Politics of Religion." *Society of Biblical Literature*. 4 April 2007. <http://www.sbl-site.org/Article.aspx?ArticleId=151>.

Singham, Mano. *Quest for Truth: Scientific Progress and Religious Beliefs*. Bloomington: Phi Delta Kappa Educational Foundation, 2000.

Sloan, Richard P. "Doctors Aren't Chaplains: The Misguided Effort to Meld Religion and Medicine." *Los Angeles Times*. 2 Dec 2006: A13.

Sokolove, Michael. "The Believer." *The New York Times Magazine*. 22 May 2005: 56+.

Sollod, Robert N. "The Hollow Curriculum." *The Academy and the Possibility of Belief: Essays on Intellectual and Spiritual Life*. Eds. Mary Louise Buley-Meissner, Mary McCaslin Thompson, and Elizabeth Bachrach Tan. Cresskill, NJ: Hampton Press, 2000.

Sontag, Susan. *Where the Stress Falls*. New York: Picador USA, 2001.

Springsteen, Bruce. Taped Interview. Rock and Roll Hall of Fame, Cleveland Ohio. 28 August 2010.

Strauch, Barbara. "How to Train the Aging Brain." *The New York Times*. 3 Jan 2010. 10 Jan 2010. <http://www.nytimes.com/2010/01/03education/edlife/03adult-t.html?hp=&pagewanted=print>.

Thorp, Holden. "Evolution's Bottom Line." *New York Times*. 12 May 2006: A27.

Works Cited

A Time to Kill. Dir. Joel Schumacher. Perf. Sandra Bullock, Samuel L. Jackson, Matthew McConaughey, Kevin Spacey. Warner Bros., 1996. Film.

Trilling, Lionel. *The Experience of Literature.* Garden City: Doubleday, 1967.

Updike, John. *Conversations with John Updike.* Ed. James Path. Jackson: University Press of Mississippi. 1994.

_____. "On Being a Self Forever." *Writing as Reflective Action: A Reader.* Eds. Duncan Carter and Sherrie Gradin. New York: Longman, 2001.

Vattimo, Gianni. *Belief.* Stanford: Stanford University Press, 1999.

Vygotsky, Lev. *Thought and Language.* Ed. Alex Kozulin. Cambridge: MIT Press, 1986.

Wagner, Joseph B. "John Updike and Karl Barth: An Insistent 'Yes.'" *Cithara.* 18.1 St. Bonaventure University Press, 1978. 61–69.

Walsh, T. M., and K. C. Diller. "Neurolinguistic Foundations to Methods of Teaching a Second Language." *International Review of Applied Linguistics.* 16 (1978): 1–14.

West, Cornel. *The American Evasion of Philosophy.* London: University of Wisconsin Press, 1989.

_____. *The Cornel West Reader.* New York: Basic Civitas Books, 1999.

White, Edmund. *Marcel Proust.* New York: Viking, 1999.

Wielenberg, Erik J. *God and the Reach of Reason: C. S. Lewis, David Hume, and Bertrand Russell.* New York: Cambridge University Press, 2008.

Woodward, Bob. *Plan of Attack.* New York: Simon & Schuster, 2004.

Index